Confessions

of a Successful

Grants Writer

A Complete Guide to Discovering and Obtaining Funding

Joanne Oppelt, MHA, GPC

Confessions

of a **Successful**

Grants Writer

A Complete Guide to Discovering
and Obtaining Funding

*Charity*Channel®

P R E S S™

Confessions of a Successful Grants Writer
One of the **In the Trenches**™ series
Published by CharityChannel Press, an imprint of CharityChannel LLC
30021 Tomas, Suite 300
Rancho Santa Margarita, CA 92688-2128 USA
http://charitychannel.com

ISBN: 978-0-9841580-5-8
Library of Congress Control Number: 2011937939

13 12 11 10 8 7 6 5 4 3 2 1

Printed in the United States of America on permanent paper.

This and most CharityChannel Press books are available at special quantity discounts for bulk purchases for sales promotions, premiums, fundraising, or educational use. For information, contact CharityChannel Press, 30021 Tomas, Suite 300, Rancho Santa Margarita, CA 92688-2128 USA. +1 949-589-5938.

About the Author

Joanne Oppelt, MHA, GPC

Joanne Oppelt has been in the field of nonprofit resource development since 1993. She is a Certified Grants Professional and a member of the Grant Professionals Association where she contributes to the association's e-newsletter. Joanne is an Adjunct Professor at Kean University in Union, New Jersey. She has conducted grant writing workshops for the Westfield United Fund and webinars for CharityChannel's CharityUniversity™ Network. She has also served on conference funding panels and has interviewed for podcasts for the Center for Nonprofit Success.

During her nine years at Community Access Unlimited, Joanne personally raised more than $9.2 million and increased agency annual operating revenues by more than $1.75 million. She published the organization's quarterly newsletter *The Independent Citizen* as well as the agency's annual report.

Joanne facilitated the funding allocation process at the March of Dimes Central Jersey Chapter, was selected to serve as a proposal reviewer for the US Department of Education Goals 2000 Initiative and has served as a grants reviewer for the Union County Department of Human Services.

Joanne holds a Bachelors of Arts in Education from Bethany University in Santa Cruz, California and a Masters in Health Administration from Wilkes University in Wilkes-Barre, Pennsylvania.

She resides in New Jersey with her husband Rick.

Connect with Joanne at
http://charitychannel.com/cc/joanne-oppelt

Acknowledgements

First off, I would like to thank those I worked for at Maternal and Family Health Services, March of Dimes Birth Defects Foundation - Central Jersey Chapter, Prevent Child Abuse – New Jersey, Family to Family Network of New Jersey, the Christian Health Care Center, and Community Access Unlimited. It is because of their training and patience with me that I have been able to hone my craft.

A special "Thank You" goes to Sid Blanchard at Community Access. He let me reach professional heights that I never knew were possible. He allowed me to push the limits of my position and encouraged me in doing so. Sid contributed greatly to my finding out what I am capable of. To him, I will always be grateful.

And to Mercedes Witowsky. Mercedes changed my life forever through her straightforwardness and steadfast fairness. She has been an important influence on me. I value what she has given me.

A special thank you for the loving assistance of all my manuscript readers who helped make the final production of this book what it is: my parents, Nate and Mary Heuberger; my husband, Rick; and my forever friend, CJ Jones. Your input was invaluable.

Most of all, none of this would have been possible without the support and encouragement of my husband, Rick. Rick has put up with the long working hours, the time away from home, and the sharing of my frustrations without complaint. Although to him grant writing is about as exciting as watching the grass grow, he has listened to me constantly talk about my craft. He has helped me see through the issues, helped me to maintain a positive perspective and helped me figure out my own solutions to perplexing problems. Because of who Rick is, I am a better person.

Thank you all.

Joanne Oppelt

Contents

Conclusion

Appendixes

Foreword

I have been involved in the grants profession for over twenty years. Naturally, I have read many professional books in my career. I loved this book. I found *Confessions of a Successful Grants Writer* practical, informative and easy to read. It is helpful to anyone who wants to increase proposal-based revenues.

In *Confessions of a Successful Grants Writer: A Complete Guide to Discovering and Obtaining Funding,* Joanne Oppelt has successfully demonstrated how to obtain governmental, corporate and foundation funding. Joanne has a keen insight into what makes different types of funders tick and how to approach them. The book thoroughly covers what it is funders are looking for and what it takes to successfully author a targeted proposal.

The practical tips provided in each chapter are right on and useful. The sidebars are very effective. The information provided in each chapter is written in a manner that is sensible. Joanne has included her wealth of experience in a way that fits nicely with each chapter. The information provided becomes user friendly as a result of the true-life experiences ("Confessions") communicated in the book. There is an added validity to the book to have a person with Joanne's history and experience as the author.

This book is an easy and worthwhile read for busy grants professionals. It provides a structured and realistic array of tips to assist persons involved in the grants industry, no matter what level of experience they have. There is practical information for beginning, intermediate and advanced levels.

After reading this book, you will have a better understanding of both the opportunities and challenges involved in being a grants professional.

Gail Vertz, GPC
Chief Executive Officer
Grant Professionals Association

Introduction

It's NOT about the money.

In all my years of asking for funding, the greatest lesson I've learned is: It is NOT primarily about the money. As of this writing, I've been writing grants for more than eighteen years and raised over $9.2 million in the last nine. Not once have I been funded because I've needed money. *How can that be?* you ask. *Isn't the whole purpose of writing a grant to get money?* Yes—but that shouldn't be the focus of your proposal. In fundraising, money is just a means to an end, not an end in and of itself. The real end is the impact you are achieving on those you serve. If you go after the money with the purpose of getting money, you will fail. Going after funding for funding's sake, your organization might well come across as one that's desperately in need and not financially strong. Long gone are the days when people gave just because you existed. Today, you need to convince donors that you are a successful organization and will be a good steward of their money. Your organization needing money does not motivate anybody.

It's the fulfilling of the mission that defines your organization and motivates others to act. Grant writing is about implementing a compelling mission. It's about meeting clearly defined community needs. It's about being the best conduit of funds among a variety of choices. It's about making the perfect match and establishing a productive relationship with a funder. It is NOT primarily about the money.

It is the mission that motivates. Mission defines what your organization is trying to do to make the world a better place. I believe that people in general want to be part of something bigger than themselves. I believe they want to make a positive impact in the world. Your organization's mission statement should tell them how to do that in broad terms. Your request for funding should tell them how they can do that in a specific way.

Grant writing is about establishing a partnership. Funders have money you need and you have programs and services to meet the need they have defined. You are a conduit for them—a way for them to achieve their desired impact on the world. They need someone to help them achieve their goals and you need their funds to do it. The relationship is set up to be a win-win situation. Looked at from that perspective, your job is to convince them you can deliver a win. You need to show them you are competent and can do what you say you can do.

You need funders. You need their time, talent or treasure. To get that, you need to meet the funders' needs. To meet their needs, you need to understand them. You need to know where they're coming from—their perspectives and motivations. So where do you start? With THEM. Get to know them as thoroughly as you can.

Notice the focus I am placing on "them." They don't need you. There are lots of good causes out there. There are other organizations that do what you do. To get the money, you need to stand out from your competition. In my experience, that means defining yourself in the funders' terms. You need to use their language and understand their perspective. You need to meet their needs, as opposed to yours.

This book will tell you how to better position your proposals among the many that funders receive. It will cover where to find what they tell you they want to know, and then what they don't tell you about what you should know. I will discuss the concept of organizational branding and its importance in getting your proposal funded. I'll talk about the questions they ask, the answers they're looking for and how to speak a language they'll understand. I will then cover how to write and present a comprehensive proposal. Finally, I will wrap up with a discussion on developing success, both at the organizational and interpersonal levels.

Each chapter will begin with a bulleted overview of its main concepts followed by a brief introduction. Throughout the chapter, you will find sidebars that add detail to the narrative, give hints on applying the principle being discussed or (blush) give a confession that will show my real-life experience relating to the discussion. The chapter is briefly concluded and ends with suggestions drawn from that chapter's subject matter.

I am a successful grants writer. In this book are the lessons I have learned over the years that have worked for me. If you do as I do, you too will raise lots of money. Good luck in your search for funding.

Chapter One

What They Tell You

IN THIS CHAPTER

···→ Finding foundation mission and funding indicators

···→ Understanding multiple corporate markets and how they affect funding requests

···→ Researching and understanding complex governmental regulations

B asically, there are three types of funders that grants writers concern themselves with: foundation, corporate and governmental. Each has its own way of communicating to the public. Your first job as a grants writer is to research your potential funders and find out what they say about themselves.

Foundations exist to meet community needs. They are interested in making sure they receive good proposals from strong organizations that can meet those needs. They want to make the biggest impact they can on a certain problem in the most cost effective way. And they want to easily sort out proposals that fit their preferences from those that do not. Therefore, many foundations find it in their best interest to publish a lot of information about themselves. They are also tax-exempt entities that must follow IRS disclosure rules. The section on discovering foundation motivators tells you where to find that published information and what to do with it.

Corporations exist to make profits. They are most interested in making strategic alliances with organizations that can further their brand. There are multiple markets corporations need to reach including the end market, the regulatory market and those in politics. The more you can help potential corporate funders make an impact in their markets, the more highly you will be perceived.

Government exists to ensure the welfare of the people. Because government is funded by taxpayers, governmental funding agencies must be transparent and fair in their allocation process. So there are usually tons of public information available. *Ad nauseum* at times. The challenge with most governmental funding is not that of finding enough information, but in researching and understanding the abundance of pertinent laws and regulations.

Discovering Foundation Motivators

For foundations, discovering their reasons for giving is relatively easy. Foundations are required by law to file an information return every year, known as the IRS Form 990-PF for private foundations and 990 for public foundations. (I'll just refer to either as 990's.) The 990 contains the foundation's mission, its board members, its funding guidelines and its funding recipients. Seeing the actual grant recipients and the amount in which they were funded helps you to discern exactly what type of organizations are funded and what the foundation's range of funding is. From this, you can figure out if you really fit a particular foundation's interest areas and what your "ask" amount should be.

For example, a foundation's guidelines might not state what its average grant is or they might give a range, say, of up to $250,000 (for example). By looking at its 990, you can see the amount of contributions actually given at that $250,000 level. You might find that it gives to only one organization at that level and the majority of its gifts are in the $15,000 to $20,000 range. You might find that the funder gives to large universities or medical centers the higher amounts and the human services agencies the smaller amounts. You might find that a national giving scope really means only New York and Florida or that giving in California means the San Francisco Bay area. You might also find that giving to homeless causes means only funding emergency food and shelter services or, conversely, that it means providing funds for constructing homes and apartments that will be affordable to people of low income who have no other long term housing options. You never know the true scope of what a foundation is looking for until you read its 990's, which is available to the public. They are a valuable research tool.

You can find 990's in a number of places. The place I like to go is the Foundation Directory online, but it is a paid subscription. I like the Foundation Directory online because it is so comprehensive and easy to use. You can search by grantmaker or you can search by grant. You can get a list of funders interested in your subject area with an all-encompassing subject list. You can further refine your search by geographic interest areas and the type of funding they provide. You can also find the 990 on GuideStar at http://www.guidestar.org. GuideStar will give you a useful profile of any organization that files a 990, and you can

> In my experience, either you invest time or money or both to get good research results. As of today, you can get a basic one month subscription to the Foundation Directory online for as little as $29.95 a month. If you're going to be pursuing a significant amount of grant funding over the next year, it's a worthwhile investment. If, however, you're a one person shop and will not be writing more than a handful of proposals a year, other research outlets might better fit your needs.

practical tip

get it for free. I find GuideStar not as easy to navigate as the Foundation Directory online, located at http://fconline.foundationcenter.org, however. Many researchers, though, find it very useful and swear by it.

In approaching foundations you need to remember that your application will probably be one of hundreds that they receive. If you don't fit their mission, don't waste your time and theirs—don't apply. Don't try to fit a square peg into a round hole. If you do apply and don't fit their guidelines, then you and your organization gain a reputation for not paying attention to your donors' needs. You present your organization as sloppy and unprepared because you have not done your research. Furthermore, you look like you're putting the dollar above your mission. The foundation world is a relatively small one and foundation officers and directors from around the country rub shoulders with one another. The last thing you want to do is alienate yourself from this group by building a bad reputation. Remember—it's not primarily about the money. Being able to make a positive impact in the world through your organization is why they will take interest in you. They want fulfilled mission.

After I begin by getting a summary profile of possible funders and I take a look at their 990's, I go to their websites, if they have one. Websites are helpful for gleaning information about funders in their own words. Besides that, you usually get tons more information. You can confirm any updates from 990 documents (the 990 might be a snapshot that is a year or more old). Usually, you can get a history of the foundations and an understanding of why the foundations exist. You can see any press releases they have. Sometimes annual reports are available to read. Sometimes foundations put out position or research papers, which can usually be found on their websites. These can be important in understanding what funders' strategies are or what their preferred solutions to stated problems are. Most importantly, the website will give you up-to-date application forms and guidelines.

If the foundation welcomes inquiries, I will also call, e-mail or write after I review its available information. If there is no website, I call or write for an application, application guidelines, annual report and any other published material the foundation might have. In deciding whether to write or call, I follow whatever procedures are outlined in whatever information about it I've been able to get my hands on. Calling or writing for information is often the first impression a foundation has of you and your organization. If you call, make sure you are prepared for questions. Know the funder as best you can. Let the foundation know you have done your research.

In whatever form you contact the foundation, you are introducing yourself and your organization to it. You need to make a good impression. Make sure that all of your communications are professional and cordial. Always respect its staff's time. It is extremely important for you to remember that you need it more than it needs you. You want to start your relationship by assuring it that you know and can meet its needs. You want to make the connection between your respective missions. You want to say how you think you might be able to meet the needs it has described. You want to thoroughly do your research beforehand so that you can show it that you will not waste its staff's time. You want it to know that you have its interests in mind and can follow directions. In short, you want to show it from the start that you can be a good conduit for its funds. It is extremely important for you to remember that grant writing doesn't start with the first call or letter. The relationship begins with the research.

Discovering Corporate Motivators

Discovering what drives corporations is a bit more complicated than with foundations. Of course, you go to their websites and read their information about their community involvement and corporate giving guidelines. But you also need to know a little bit about marketing and branding. This is not a book about marketing and branding. But suffice it to say, you should know enough about marketing to understand what corporate funder markets are—and there might be more than one. And you want to understand how their aligning with you will positively impact their reputations in their markets and ultimately help them increase their market share, which leads them to higher profits. Corporations and corporate foundations don't give to nonprofits purely out of the goodness of their hearts. They give because it benefits them or their business. You must understand their brand within their markets to really understand what will make you attractive to them. So, how do you do that?

First of all, you need to determine who their end customers are, that is, who purchases their goods or services. Do you meet the needs of this market? For example, TJX Companies markets its line to women and children. Does your organization help better the lives of women and children? By partnering with you, will it help the company be seen as doing more than just selling products to its market? In other words, what value added do you bring to the company in the eyes of the consumers? Usually, the end market is the easiest to understand and know because it will be obvious in the company's public relations materials who the target consumers are. You will generally have a good idea of the needs of that market if you have done your needs assessment properly.

But the end customer is not the only market that corporations target. There are also regulatory markets. Companies must live within certain legal restrictions. Do you know what the regulatory environment is? Do you know what legal restrictions the company must abide by in distributing money? Are you aware of any upcoming or recent changes that will affect the marketplace in which the company operates? Let me give you a couple of examples.

Recently, energy suppliers were deregulated, that is, energy suppliers are now allowed to be separate from energy distributors. This means a proliferation of energy-supply companies have come out of the woodwork. And they are all competing with each other for customers. They need to get their names out to as many people as possible in the least amount of time as possible, preferably with the names of people or organizations that are credible in the community. What better vehicle is there than nonprofit donor lists? The company can reach a lot of potential customers in partnership with an organization that has some credibility with those customers. The energy suppliers can present a win-win situation: giving money to a cause that is important to your donors while saving money on their energy bills. This situation is ripe for raising money from the energy-supply company. In this situation, you have a substantial advantage in the fundraising game. The question is not whether you are a good partner or not for the supply company. Instead, the question becomes one of whether you want to partner with it and whether you want your name associated with its product.

Another example of needing to know the regulatory environment is when you ask for money from banks. Banks are highly regulated. One of those regulations is the Community Reinvestment Act. The Community Reinvestment Act, or CRA, dictates how much banks must make in loans, engage in pro bono activities and give in charitable contributions and loans to people or organizations who serve people of low to moderate income. Banks are rated on how well they meet CRA requirements—the higher the rating, the better it is for them with their regulators. That means that banks that don't meet CRA standards will be looking to boost their scores, i.e., engage in more charitable activities. Do you read banks' annual reports to know how they rate? I do. And as a result, I have increased funding to my organization by hundreds of thousands of dollars: almost $350,000 over six years.

The regulators are not the only secondary market corporations care about. There are also the people who make the regulations—generally, the legislators. Because of the nature of their work, many nonprofits have very strong relationships with their local legislators—something a corporation might not have. Do local legislators come to your events? When you publicize your grant contributors, will legislators see it? Do you have a project that needs funding that involves your local government officials that a company would be interested in? In other words, can association with you help a company meet the people who make the regulations? Can the company make a positive impression on a legislator through you? Do you invite local businesses and legislators to your events?

In looking for corporate funding, it often helps if you are a customer of theirs. Don't forget about the vendors your organization does business with, including bankers, attorneys, accountants and office suppliers. These are people who often have multiple corporate connections. In addition to considering your vendors as possible donors, you can consider them as possible conduits for helping you expand your organization's market reach.

practical tip

Of course, sending out individual donor solicitations and inviting legislators and business people to organizational events is beyond the scope of pure grant writing. But knowing the regulatory environment is extremely relevant to improving the chances for your success at getting funded. It gives you an edge as you better understand the funders' needs. And there are numerous opportunities to mix what you know about the needs of your corporate and corporate foundation funders into other organizational activities.

Discovering Government Motivators

Government funders are easy to understand in the sense that there is usually plenty of public information available about them. It is legislated that government agencies have an open and fair funding process that includes public input. The information, however, is not always easy to find and can be very time consuming to look for. You might have a lot of information to dig through.

For federal grants, usually grant competitions are announced through a notice of funding availability, or NOFA. You can find NOFA's in the Federal Register, which you can receive daily through a listserve, through the grants.gov website or through an individual federal agency's website.

Sometimes NOFA's come in parts and with some time between them. For example, HUD will publish a NOFA's General Section often several months before it publishes specific program NOFA guidelines. Both NOFA sections will apply to your application. I have found, however, that Department of Education, Department of Energy, Department of Labor, Department of the Treasury and Department of Health and Human Services NOFA's are pretty self-contained in one document. That doesn't mean you'll find all applicable rules and regulations in the NOFA. It means you'll find all the application guidelines usually in one place. Your budget and contract guidelines might be found in separate Office of Management and Budget Circulars. Department of Education grants are also ruled by EDGAR, the Education Department Guidelines and Regulations. You should be familiar with all applicable regulations and publications before you start writing your applications to make sure your programs' methodology and budget address all the guidelines they need to.

In my experience, state and local governmental grants are much easier to put together. I also find that the more local the governmental unit, the more accessible the staff is if you have questions. In all government grants, though, you need to understand that a fair amount of funding is passed from the federal government to the state government and from the state to local governmental entities. You might have more or fewer layers to dig through depending on the legislation driving the funding and how densely populated your jurisdiction is.

All public funding is from tax revenues, mandated fees or the public sale of bonds. That means that allocation of this funding is dictated by legislation. Get a copy of these laws and study them. Understand the purpose of the legislation. Understand who makes the funding decisions and what the process will be. Know all the rules BEFORE you decide if you want to go for the funding. Know what you're getting into before you put 100 or more hours in writing an application. You don't want to end up spending precious time applying for an application that doesn't meet ALL the funding requirements. Sometimes the paperwork and reporting requirements add more cost to the overhead than the grant provides. Is your organization leveraged enough to be able to afford this?

Getting copies of all the pertinent legislation is not always easy. Sometimes you must look beyond what legislation has just been passed. Today's legislation is based on previous legislation which is then again based on even more previous legislation. For example, the Neighborhood Stabilization Program (NSP) is governed by Community Development Block Grant laws. To fully understand all the regulations surrounding NSP funding, you need not only to get a copy of the legislation authorizing the Neighborhood Stabilization Program statute, you also need to go back to 1974 to when the Community Development Block grant was passed. In that legislation, you find the prevailing wage laws governing the Community Development Block Grant were written in the 1940's in another piece of legislation. You cannot understand the intricacies of the NSP funding guidelines without understanding all this previous legislation and its requirements.

Researching and digging through all those laws for pertinent regulations is an extremely time consuming task. It can take you hours. But it is essential to fully understanding what you

> Community development projects include building affordable housing. Housing projects can be particularly vexing. Not only do you have funding regulations to concern yourself with, you also have zoning laws, environmental regulations and building codes that you need to be aware of. I have heard of horror stories where an agency purchased land and paid architects for plans only to have the site be environmentally unsound or the proposed development did not abide by existing zoning codes. Although these challenges were eventually overcome, it was only at considerable cost and political capital.
>
> **watch out!**

are getting yourself into. I have heard story after story of nonprofit organizations having to go back to the drawing board with architects or planning boards or town councils because they started the project one way and the regulations require a different way. An organization can spend a lot of precious financial and political capital very quickly by not knowing ALL the regulations up front.

And then, knowing the laws is not enough. You must also be aware of the interpretations of all those laws. This is where governmental program staff are very helpful. If you are fortunate, the agency promulgating the funding has written guides with questions and answers to understanding the funding rules. The guides are very helpful, but again, time-consuming to dig through. The good news is that all of this information is public and pretty accessible. The bad news is that it takes time—a lot of time.

So the lesson here is to be aware of the different purposes each type of funder exists for and the effects that has on the types of public information you can find. Information is out there. It just takes know how to get to it.

To Recap

◆ Read and review 990's.

◆ Match your mission to that of the funder.

◆ Align your corporate requests with the needs of their markets.

◆ Be aware of regulatory and political environments.

◆ Read through all parts of a NOFA and its applicable guidelines.

◆ Research and understand all applicable legislation.

Chapter Two

What They Don't Tell You

IN THIS CHAPTER

- ···→ Presenting a professional-grade funding request
- ···→ Dealing with program officers
- ···→ Presenting your organization as a good corporate partner
- ···→ Managing differences in corporate culture
- ···→ Dealing with legislators and government staffers

Grant writing is persuasive in nature: You are trying to persuade someone to make a decision to fund you. To influence decision-making effectively, you need to understand how funders make decisions and in what context they make them. This information is not usually written down, much less published. In this chapter, we will cover the ins and outs of understanding who makes the funding calls within each type of funder and how you can best impact those funding decisions.

First of all, let me tell you where I am coming from as a grants reviewer. On a foundation level, I once worked as a program officer for a local chapter of a national foundation. On a governmental level, I have reviewed grants at both the national and county level. I have never been involved in decision-making in a corporation, but the person who helped me craft my corporate informational materials was a corporate community relations officer in an international company in charge of allocating corporate donations. She has been instrumental in helping me formulate my strategy in approaching corporations for support. And it's worked.

Foundation Perspectives

Foundations are run by boards of directors who carry out the founder's mission as they interpret it. These board members are generally well-educated professionals; lawyers, bankers, accountants, corporate executives, and sometimes public officials are fairly common. Your proposal should be written at a business professional level, about twelfth grade in vocabulary and reading level. It should also look like a professional business document. Looking professional does not mean a bound presentation with a glossy cover. Looking professional means a presentation that is typewritten with plenty of white space on the page, no spelling errors and no math errors.

The document also needs to be consistent with itself: What's described in the methodology is what's asked for in the budget, the numbers in the proposal narrative match the numbers in the budget, and the outcomes you describe relate to the issues you are trying to solve and the needs you outline. These are simple guidelines, but breaking them is a common mistake in proposals.

It is always surprising to me that almost all funders have war stories of unprofessional proposals they receive: proposals addressed to the wrong foundation, unsigned cover letters, and budget numbers that don't add up or that differ from the proposal narrative. One foundation representative even remarked to his audience how he has received handwritten proposals. Needless to say, none of these potential grantees got far in their quest.

watch out!

Make sure the goals of your proposal are in line with the funder's goals and that all the major concepts in your proposal relate to them. For example, say that you need funding for the youth in foster care you work with so that they can present their experiences in conference settings to professionals who work with at-risk youth. Further, say you are writing to a foundation whose goal is to improve the psychological welfare of youth. You will want to phrase your proposal in terms that reflect the goal of the foundation. In other words, your goal for the project will not be to provide for transportation costs, it will be to improve the emotional and mental health of at-risk youth. Your needs statement, then, will not talk about the high cost of providing such opportunities to the youth, but the psychological benefits of abused or neglected youth telling their story. In this case, you will need to cite psychological research to substantiate your point. You might also want to cite best practices in the field regarding such presentations and the exponential impact such presentations can have. Your objectives, in turn, will address improvements in mental health and contribution to best practices and your evaluation will measure such objectives. We will talk in detail about how to make sure the different parts of your proposal relate to the funder's objectives in Chapter Three. And we will discuss maintaining consistency throughout the proposal in Chapters Four and Five.

You also want to understand how foundation board members think and organize information. You can do this is a variety of ways: through Foundation Directory or other summary profiles, foundation websites, annual reports, research studies, position papers, press releases and, of course, application guidelines. The more of any of these you can get and read, the better off you are. By reading literature foundations publish, you will be better able to understand and use their language, identify their issues and understand their approach to solving problems. If you're lucky, they've put out research or position papers that you can use to justify your ask. In other words, you will be able to reach them where they are. You will communicate to them that you understand them, which lays the foundation for a trusting relationship. And if they feel they can trust you, your chances of funding just went up exponentially.

For example, the MacArthur Foundation

> Every profession has its own jargon and language. Although you don't want to use jargon, you will want to use language common within the professional context your proposal addresses. You do want to come across as versant in the field.

practical tip

funds community development projects. They are particularly concerned about the current shortage of affordable rental housing. MacArthur has sponsored studies and put out research that substantiates this issue. I use its research in my housing applications. It gives me credibility to be able to back up my position with national statistics that are validated by a well-respected player in the field. Certainly, I will use this research in applications to other community development funding sources. I will especially make sure to use MacArthur's research if I am applying to the MacArthur Foundation itself or if I am applying to another foundation that partners with MacArthur. Using a foundation's own research communicates to the foundation's board members—the funding decision-makers—that I am definitely a partner that has the same interests and goals as they do. It is a big first step in the process of making that perfect match between this funder and my organization.

As far as application guidelines go—ALWAYS FOLLOW THE FUNDER'S RULES. This might sound simple, but it's the number one rule that's broken. If it wants one page, don't give it more. If it has a preferred format, follow it. Answer all its questions. If your program doesn't fit in with its priorities, don't apply. Foundation board members are a pretty small, close knit group and they talk to each other. You do not want to get the reputation that you can't follow directions or that your organization is desperately chasing money. If you can't or won't follow directions, it calls into question whether you will be able to comply with contract and reporting requirements. If you're desperately chasing money, you call into question your organization's management and viability. Either way, you lose.

I can't emphasize it enough: *Always follow the rules of the funder.*

important

One more thing about larger foundations: they have program officers. It is the program officer's job to make sure that the board has a field of good choices in which to make decisions. That means the program officer is your friend—it is in the program officer's best interest that you submit a good proposal. A program officer will actually help you submit a good proposal. So, if you have questions, ask the program officer. It is always a good idea to introduce yourself and your organization to a program officer, if the foundation accepts phone calls or emails. Contact them in the way they say they want to be contacted. And it is very important not to wait until the last minute to contact them. Most proposals are written just before deadline. You don't want to wait until the last minute for two reasons: you don't want to impose on the funders when they are at their busiest and you don't want to present yourself or your organization as going by the seat of your pants with no strategy or planning behind you. If you do these things, you come across as unfocused and poorly managed. Remember—prior planning prevents poor performance.

Corporate Perspectives

As opposed to foundations, the board of directors of corporations are not accountable to a mission. They are accountable to stockholders. Stockholders are interested in profit. The primary motivation around corporations is profit. Always remember this.

Usually in a larger corporation there is a community relations person who is in charge of allocating corporate contributions, among other things. It is this person's job to make sure the company has a solid public image. This means that businesses nowadays want to be seen as involved with and helping their communities. Strong communities mean better business.

So to make a mark in the corporate funding arena, you want to be seen as a good partner. That means you must have a good brand, that is, a strong reputation in the community for achieving the goals you set out to do. You need to think of your organization the way a businessperson thinks of his or her business—*what do I have to offer my consumers that sets me apart from my competitors?* And it's not just the end user of our services that is our consumer. In the nonprofit world you have multiple constituencies: clients, funders, regulators and the community at large. As we saw in Chapter One, corporate funders are savvy at dealing with multiple constituencies. You need to be, too.

Corporate executives are used to dealing with business concepts and financial viability issues. They are experts in communicating their competitive advantages to their customers. To be perceived to be on top of your game to a corporation, then, you need to be concerned with the same issues they are. Questions to ask yourself *before* the corporate funder asks them are:

❑ Am I successful? How do I know?

❑ Is my business profitable? Do I run in the black? What else do my financial indicators say about me?

❑ Will I be around in five years? How do I know? What is my plan?

❑ Do I have strong leadership? Who makes the final decisions and why is he or she qualified to do so?

❑ Am I well managed? Who is our management team?

❑ What makes my organization unique? How am I different than others like me?

❑ What kind of environment do I operate in? What are the risks? What are the opportunities?

❑ Who is my competition? On what basis do we compete?

❑ Who are my partners? What makes them good partners? How does that partnership help me achieve success?

These are the types of questions corporate executives must answer to their stockholders about their companies. In turn, they should be the type of questions you should answer for them. You are partners of theirs. How is helping you helping them? How can you be an asset to them reaching their goals?

But executives are busy people. They live in very fast-paced environments and are constantly pummeled with information. They want to be able to digest what you have to say very quickly. Which means short and easy to read. Pictures, charts and graphs work well. And generally, you have one page for each idea you are trying to communicate with no more than five pages to a packet, preferably three. If you're limited to one page with pictures and charts with plenty of white space, you will not have a lot of room for text. The challenge is to be succinct and to the point without coming across as brusque or jarring. It takes a lot of work to do this well. You might go through several drafts.

As you might have figured out, I am not talking anymore about traditional proposal writing. What I am talking about, really, is developing corporate marketing materials. In my experience, the first step to developing a corporate contributions proposal is working on your marketing pitch.

Corporations will want to know about your organization and your organization's health before they ask about your need. They want to position themselves as successful and want to partner with successful nonprofits. That helps their image. In-depth discussions about marketing are beyond the scope of this book. For recommended resources, see *Appendix C.*

Once you have materials ready for them, you have to get their attention. But how? Hundreds of people are trying to get their attention and giving away money is not one of their priorities—making a profit is. In my experience the most effective way to get corporate executives' attention is to network with them. Attend events they will attend. For example, is the executive of the corporation being honored by any community groups? Who is selling tickets to the event? Will you be there? Is the executive active on any nonprofit boards? Which ones? What events do those nonprofits hold? Is the business active in its local Chamber of Commerce? Are there any Chamber networking groups you can join? Are you involved in their events?

In communicating with business executives, you also need to be aware of differences in corporate culture between your organization and theirs. Most, not all, business executives are on the conservative side of things—the way they dress, their social norms and their political views. Conversely, most, not all, nonprofits are on the more liberal side of things—they are more informal in their attire, there's generally a family feel to the organizational environment and they politically lean a little more towards the left. Of course, there are exceptions. In any case, you will have two separate organizational cultures and value systems.

> One of the tenets in advertising is name recognition. Advertisers pay dearly to make sure their product names are regularly communicated to the consumer. You need to make sure you get a corporate executive's attention—your consumer in this case. The more you can get your organization's name in front of a corporation, the better off you are. Networking pays off big.

practical tip

How do you meld these cultures while maintaining organizational integrity? Well, don't ask them to change. They will be offended if you ask them to be like you or incorporate your points of view. What you need to do is understand their world as they see it. There are a myriad of ways to do this, including reading the paper—especially the business section —every day, subscribing to regular business publications and joining professional or educational groups such as Toastmasters International, The Drucker Institute or The American Association of University Women. Accept them as they are and meet them where they are. Focus on mutual goals rather than the differences you have in meeting those goals.

For example, I am currently active in a local regional Chamber of Commerce. I started working with it so that I could network with area businesses. I quickly learned just how diverse our respective world views were. Our solutions to societal problems were radically different. I believed in investing in a strong social safety net through tax allocations; they believed that investing through government wasted taxpayer dollars. I knew right away I needed help. So I started reading the business section of our statewide paper to keep up on the news of what was going on in the corporate world, to know what issues they were dealing with and to gain an understanding of their perspectives. I also subscribed to a statewide business publication, NJ Biz, to do the same thing. I learned where we similar: We both wanted strong, healthy, vibrant communities. They wanted stronger communities so that they could attract good employees with attractive places to live, increase product production and raise the skill level of their workforce. We both wanted to keep people who were homeless off the street. We both wanted job creation. We both wanted higher literacy rates, graduation rates and educational attainment. I had a solution to some of their business needs. And I presented myself as a good business partner because I presented my organization in language they understood.

So now you are armed with information about your organization that is communicated in ways the corporate executive can digest it, you understand their issues and you've gotten their attention. What else do you need to do to ask corporations for money?

In my experience, persistence is vital. You will not get anywhere without persistence. As I've stated before, corporate executives are busy people and giving away money is not one of their priorities. Do not be discouraged if they say they will get back to you and never do. Do not be afraid to feel like you are pestering them. If you have a relationship with them, they will get to you when their priorities allow. Usually that's a long time. So if they forget about you, don't be afraid to remind them that you're still there. But ALWAYS be respectful of their time, no matter how many times they've put you off. You are trying to convince them you are a good partner. How you handle frustration tells them a lot.

Governmental Perspectives

Government funders are not accountable to boards of directors or stockholders. They are accountable to the taxpayers and the political system in which funding decisions are made. Understanding how the political system works is crucial to getting governmental funding.

> It once took me two years to get an appointment with a particular company. I met the director of community relations at a community event his company hosted. Two years of regular phone calls went by and I almost gave up. But then, in part because I wouldn't go away and was nice about it and in part because my organization has a successful business strategy that I presented in corporate terms, he took me out to lunch and we talked. Next thing I knew, my organization was part of his charitable giving budget for the upcoming year. That was several years ago. I now have a relationship with him where I call every year to see at what amount we are in his budget. Of course, I'm more subtle than that. And I give him back things too. For example, I have volunteer activities for his workforce and I do public speaking to the youth with which his company works. The relationship is a business one: one of two partners working together. We both benefit. It is a win-win relationship.

Let's start with politicians who make the laws. Politicians are elected into office by voters. Politicians maintain their jobs by keeping voters happy. Their political parties also help them get elected as each party works to influence voters. The more politicians of one party who get elected, the more power that party has. Interest groups also affect elections as they provide a significant amount of the money that allows the politician to run a campaign and reach as many voters as possible. So, when you are approaching a politician about a funding decision, you need to take into account the perspectives of all these constituencies—voters, political parties and interest groups.

You need to deliver a win for politicians. You need to create jobs or provide housing or improve the quality of life in some way. Your project needs to be in line with what the politicians promised the voters. Most of all, though, you need to improve the politicians' brand just as you do with corporate partners. You need to give them positive visibility with their constituencies. They need to see you as someone who makes them look effective, as someone who helps the community they represent be a better place to live.

Accomplishing this means visiting legislators and getting to know their staff. Send them your newsletters and annual reports so they can see what you do in the community. Keep abreast of what bills they proposed and where they stand on the issues so that you can be a resource for them. One of your organization's strengths and your strength as a grants writer is that you specialize in whatever subject matter you and your organization are involved in and that someone in your organization works directly with the public. You probably have much more in-depth knowledge of a particular area or the needs of a particular constituency than the legislators do just because you work with that population every day. Can you help legislators understand an issue better? Send them a letter with a research article addressing that topic. Invite politicians for site visits so they can see your impact in the community.

What is your relationship with the community? How does the public perceive you? How involved are you with the public? Can you invite legislators to speak to your constituency or help them otherwise reach the voters? Be careful, though, if you do this. If you receive governmental funding, there are laws against lobbying that you must be aware of. You do not want to jeopardize your organization's nonprofit status.

Although a nonprofit can advocate on many issues, there are strict rules against what kind of activities a nonprofit can engage in within the confines of its funding and tax-exempt status. Generally, a nonprofit with governmental funding can educate its constituencies about candidates or legislation and they can conduct voter drives but they cannot directly lobby legislators or influence elections. To be safe, use revenue other than that of governmental funding when dealing with political issues.

watch out!

Good governmental grants writers need to know what is going on in the political environment around them so they know when to advance their cause. They need to be astute to the needs of legislators. Getting legislators' attention can help you further your agenda. But first, you need to further theirs.

Another one of your target groups is government workers. Most civil servants have job security. They are, for the most part, not worried about keeping their jobs. Instead, they are worried about following and implementing the rules and regulations enacted by the politicians. They are the gatekeepers and enforcers. This is why governmental staff are really helpful to you in preparing an application. If you get funded, they will have to monitor you. They want the fewest problems possible from the start to reduce the amount of future problems they might face. This is a win-win for you. Governmental program staff want good proposals that follow all the rules. Usually, there is more than enough help in preparing adequate applications, from webinars to conference calls to one-on-one technical assistance. Government staffers can be your best friends when applying for governmental funding. Use them. Listen to them. They are there to help you.

Most of your contact with governmental program staffers comes after you are funded. They need to make sure that public funds are spent wisely and in the manner for which they were approved. The easier you can make their job, the better. ALWAYS send in your reports on time. If there is a change to the scope of what you originally proposed, inform them immediately. Remember, they want you to succeed. Taking money back causes all sorts of bureaucratic nightmares they'd rather not have to resolve. So don't make

> Asking your questions about what the rules mean and how to follow them BEFORE reporting begins makes life easier and smooths the relationship with the governmental staffers.
>
>  practical tip

them your enemies by arguing with them. Yes, the government can be picky and some of what they ask for might not make much sense to you. Do it anyway—do what they ask. Government program staffers work in a political bureaucracy. They need to make their bosses, the politicians, look good. Help them do that in any way you can.

So we've talked about the different perspectives that motivate different types of funders. Astute grants writers understand the audience to whom they are writing and present information in a way that that audience best comprehends. You must present yourself and your organization as a good partner to multiple constituencies, no matter who the funder.

To Recap

◆ Always follow the rules of the funder.

◆ Present your request in ways the funder best comprehends.

◆ Be attentive to your brand.

◆ Utilize available funding staff to give you an edge.

◆ Be persistent.

◆ Be respectful of differences.

Chapter Three

Why They Would Choose Your Organization

IN THIS CHAPTER

---→ The importance of matching missions

---→ Building a strong organizational brand

---→ The role of values and vision statements

---→ Where do we find donors for our campaign?

---→ Playing off your organization's strengths and addressing your organization's weaknesses

Successful proposals answer the question of why your organization is worthy of funders' resources, i.e., what makes you one of the best partners out there. Funders receive far more requests than they can fulfill and most of the requests are for worthy causes. So how do you position *your* proposal so that it is at the head of the pack?

What I find helpful is to think of what I am trying to do for my organization beyond the scope of one grant. In other words, I have a strategy in mind and know how I want to be seen in the funding marketplace. I position my organization in that total marketplace as opposed to just one funder.

Why do I take such a broad approach? Because what I am doing is building a reputation, or brand. There are a finite number of funders out there and they're a pretty small group. They talk to each other. I want them to notice me before I submit an application. It gives me a valuable and important edge. And in the world of extremely competitive funding, I need all the edge I can get.

Meeting Their Needs: Matching Missions

In a true partnership, each side gives and gets something. You need to give funders what they need to meet their goals in order to get their funding. Notice it is what *they* need, not what *you* need. If you talk about them meeting your needs without first letting them how you will meet their needs, it is not a true partnership.

The first step in meeting their needs is matching your mission to theirs. This does not mean that you change your mission statement to be like theirs. Again, funders are a relatively small group of people and you don't want people to get confused about who your organization is and what your organization does. The trick, instead, is to be able to describe facets of yourself in the overall context of who you are.

> You need a strong organizational identity in a competitive marketplace. As such, your organizational mission never changes. I always state our organizational mission in every proposal I write, no matter what the funder's mission is. However, each program our organization operates has its own goals. So I spend time highlighting the program goals that best match the mission of the funder in addition to stating my organizational mission.

practical tip

Try to think of this way. You are a Rubik's Cube. You are proud to be a Rubik's Cube. You are the best Rubik's Cube around. But the funder wants to fund yellow. Well, as a cube you have six different sides. One of them happens to be yellow. You can still be true to your mission of being a Rubik's Cube while describing the one program of yours that is yellow. You maintain integrity to your mission while matching yourself to what it's looking for.

To put it in more concrete terms, say that you are an organization that deals with domestic violence, specifically spousal. Most of the people you support are women and children. What types of funders can you pursue? Obviously, those that deal directly with domestic violence programs. As families flee their abusers, they need their basic needs met—so you will probably also meet the guidelines of some funder's need whose goal is to meet basic human needs. If you provide emergency shelter, you fall under housing and community development. Funders dealing with affordable housing and temporary shelter might be interested in you. You're probably also providing counseling services to women and children so you fall under mental health. The children will need their educational needs met until they are relocated; if you have any sort of on-site educational program, you're going to fall under education. Since you're dealing with children, you'll also fall under children and youth services. And so on. Not once in all these possibilities have I veered from my organization's mission. I have just addressed the myriad of different programs the organization has.

It is important that you maintain integrity with your mission. You want to be seen as a strong organization who knows who it is and where it's going. You want to appear successful. You want funders to know you can do what you say you can do. Adhering to your mission is your first step.

Building Their Trust: A Strong Organizational Brand

The mission tells the world what the organization does. The brand tells the world if the organization actually does it. It is my organization's brand that defines the perceptions of who my organization is as opposed to who I say it is. Branding the organization as a whole goes beyond proposal writing and is the subject of multiple other books on the market. However, good grants writers know how to brand their organization through their craft.

A brand, put in simple terms, is your reputation. It defines what you stand for. It shapes others' expectations of what you can and cannot deliver. It builds trust. You say, "This is my promise," and your brand says, "Here's how we think you perform in delivering on that promise."

The value of many corporate brands is calculated and stated using a monetary value. A brand value can then be used in a company's financial statements and is often used when valuing a company's selling price. Strong brands are highly-sought commodities. Their importance cannot be overstated.

practical tip

Branding has a lot to do with proposal writing. In a proposal, you are trying to convince funders that your organization can deliver a win. You want them to know that your organization can deliver on its promises. Funders, whether foundation, corporate or governmental, have promises to keep as well. They want to know how well your organization can help them deliver a win. They want to be associated with organizations that have positive brand images.

Put in sales terms, submitting a proposal is like selling a product. That product is your program. You are trying to improve sales of your product—in this case, attract funding. The more "buyers" you can get, the more funding you generate. How do you entice buyers to try your product? How do you separate your organization from the rest of the pack? In other words, how do you define your organization's brand?

The most common reason proposals get rejected is because they do not fit the priorities of the funder or because they're sloppy. You want to brand yourself and your organization positively. The basic rules to follow are simple but are also the most often broken. Follow the rules of the funder. Make sure your proposal is consistent with what it is asking. Make sure what you are trying to do is what it's trying to do. Tailor each application to that specific funder's needs. Do your homework and know what those needs are. Use its language. Use its format. Be consistent: Make sure the narrative and the budget tell the same story. Check for spelling errors and typos. Check the addition in your budget. Don't make these common mistakes. They'll kill your request. If you can't manage a simple request, how can a funder trust you to manage its money?

Strong proposals are consistent within themselves. We will talk about how to achieve this kind of consistency in Chapters Four and Five. In the larger context, however, you must not only be consistent within your proposal, you must also present your organization as consistent with itself. You want to maintain a strong organizational identity.

The mission defines who the organization is. You must make sure that what you write is consistent with the organization's mission. This, again, sounds simple but it is often more difficult than it looks. Nonprofits in need of money often go after all the funding they can, no matter who it's from or what it's for. If their organization sort of, kind of fits the funding guidelines, they will apply. This is a serious mistake. Going after money for money's sake often leads to mission drift. Mission drift is when an organization veers a little off course. The organization starts concentrating on its peripheral activities as opposed to its core activities. It starts violating its own core values.

This is NOT how you want to be perceived in the marketplace. If your organization experiences mission drift, your organization will be not be perceived as trustworthy. The organization will not be able to deliver on its promise of why it says it exists. The organization will not be perceived as well managed. People will be confused and not know what the organization stands for. The organization will not have a clearly-defined brand. A muddled brand does not make a good match for funders; it does not help the funders promote their brand or meet their objectives. An organization must ALWAYS stick to its mission. It is the basic building block of who that organization is.

Your mission is not the only thing that defines your organization; your organization's values also do. What are your organization's core values? How are those values expressed? Organizational values help explain why the organization does what it does in the way that it does it. Values statements are strong statements to make. Stating and adhering to values shows organizational integrity. The other component that defines your organization is its vision. The board is responsible for defining the organization's vision and the executive director is responsible for infusing that vision to the staff. Organizations that function in a concerted and cohesive effort have strong organizational identities: Everyone is on the same page and working for the same goal. Vision is crucial to moving an organization forward. Mission gives us the "what" of what we do. Values gives us the "why" of how we do it. Vision tells us what we're striving for.

> Savvy organizations, both for-profit and nonprofit, develop values and vision statements in addition to mission statements.
>
>
> practical tip

Are your organization's values evident in your proposal? Is your narrative consistent with those values and beliefs? Is everyone associated with the organization striving toward the same goals? These are important issues to address. An organization that comes across as consistent with its values with everyone moving to the same tune is perceived as a strong organization. And strong organizations are perceived as more favorable partners.

Being strong on vision and values can also make up for other measurements of success that might not be as strong. For example, you don't have to have a big budget to be an organization with strong direction and organizational integrity. You can also be a relatively new organization and still be a top contender because you know where you're going and how you're going to get there.

Citing your organization's values and demonstrating that your program operates by them is not enough, however. You need to show consistency with those values THROUGHOUT your proposal. For example, if you are helping people to meet basic needs, does your budget show that your organization gives its workers enough hours and pays them fair wages to be able to do the same? If access to health care is your issue, what kind of benefits does your organization provide? If you are integrating people into the community, do you show how important community groups contribute to what you're doing? Who are your other funders? What will that list show? It's not enough that you do your job and write a good proposal. Your supporting documentation must show consistency between your organization's values and your organization's operating activities.

Playing Off Your Organization's Strengths

Organizations, like people, have strengths and weaknesses. We all know that. In trying to convince funders that our organization is the best conduit for their funds, we brag about our organization's strengths. We talk about how the organization measures up against like organizations. We tell others about what awards or citations the organization has won, how robust the budget is, how many community connections the agency has, how experienced the staff is, how the organization is growing, how many people the agency supports. The list is endless. We do this to appear successful.

But it is equally important to be aware of and talk about our organization's weaknesses. Not that we want to brag about our agency's weaknesses or put the focus on what the agency can't do. All organizations have weakness. When you show that your agency is aware of its weaknesses, that in and of itself is a strength. If your organization is aware of its weaknesses, it has the power and ability to do something about them. A strong organization will show it uses its strengths to compensate for its weaknesses.

For example, are you a small organization with a small budget and small staff? Turn that around to show what a great collaborator you are and how you can bring multiple perspectives together to achieve a common goal. Show what skills you have in place to accomplish this and how much bigger that makes your impact. Is your cause controversial? Show how the organization is supporting a special constituency or providing a service that is needed that no one else offers. Did your executive director just leave? Talk about the transition strategy of your board and the leadership capabilities of your agency's senior staff. Weaknesses are only opportunities waiting to happen. The trick in discussing weaknesses is to acknowledge them, discuss them and address how you are dealing with them.

Strengths and weaknesses are also interpreted by their context. Every organization operates within a constantly changing environment. What was perceived as a strength yesterday might be perceived as a weakness today. For example, if you work for an organization that has a well known liberal or conservative leaning, your organization will be perceived as an asset or a liability depending on the political party in power. That, in turn, affects what might or might not be funded. Always be aware of the political environment in which you're operating. Try to understand what the deliverables are and find common ground. You can then position yourself accordingly. You want to be perceived as a friend by those who make decisions. Help them deliver a win no matter what their political philosophy is.

But it's not only the political environment that you need to take into account. The economy has a big effect too, as we can see from the recent recession. What was perceived as necessary when times were good can be seen as lavish now. Again, I go back to your budget. Are your salaries in line with those in your field? Are your other expenses in line with what the current market can bear? How do you know? Are you leveraging your resources? Do you have in-kind contributions? Do you have wide community support? Are you asking for only what you need or are you padding your budget? In every review session I've ever sat on, there has always been at least one person who has questioned every expense in the budget. Can your budget survive that kind of scrutiny?

And it's not only in your budget that you must demonstrate these things. Most funders want to know what will happen if they don't support you and, if they do support you, how you are going to continue the program when their funding ends. If you're a strong organization, they want to know why you are asking them for money. If you're struggling, they want to know how they can be sure you'll be around tomorrow. So what's the solution? It seems like a no-win situation. If you're showing a healthy bottom line, why should they fund you when there are so many struggling organizations out there? And if you're barely scraping by, how do they know their funding will lead to long term results?

That's why it is important for you to address mission rather than money. Talk about impact. If your organization is strong, funders are making an investment in the future. Funding your organization guarantees a long-term, leveraged impact. If you're barely scraping by, talk about what you have done, the community needs you meet and your plan to address your current challenges. Talk about how success in meeting past needs has prepared your organization for the current crisis. Openly talk about the threats your agency faces. Funders are pretty smart people and know what the landscape out there is. Address the threats they know are there. But turn the threats into positives; see them as opportunities. Talk about your readiness to meet your threats. Talk about the skills and expertise your organization possesses that will positively position your organization's ability to meet your coming challenges.

In the crowded nonprofit world, you want to stand out as an excellent partner. You want to show you can deliver a win in meeting the funder's needs. You want to create a strong organizational identity and strong positive brand. Maintaining consistency between your proposal and your organization's mission, values and vision does that. Addressing your organization's weakness through its strengths also shows organizational strength.

To Recap

◆ To show you can meet the needs of funders, match your mission and program goals to theirs.

◆ Maintain integrity by adhering to your mission, values and vision.

◆ Address your weaknesses by playing off your strengths.

Chapter Four

The Eight Questions They Want Answered

IN THIS CHAPTER

- ···→ Describing the true need

- ···→ Talking about your program

- ···→ Defining and measuring success

- ···→ Presenting costs

- ···→ The importance of showing community support

- ···→ Showing leverage and sustainability

There are eight questions all funders want answered, whether or not they explicitly ask for the information. As a grants writer, it is your job to anticipate their questions and address their concerns. In this chapter, I will outline the eight questions I always explore in my proposal narrative and the techniques I use in crafting their answers.

The eight questions every funder needs answered are:

1. What need are you meeting?

2. How are you going to meet it?

3. How will you know if you are successful?

4. How will you measure that?

5. How much will it cost?

6. Do you have community support?

7. How will you sustain your efforts?

8. What makes your organization uniquely qualified to do what you propose?

What need are you meeting?

Of course, you write proposals because your organization needs funding. But that's not what funders are looking for. Long gone are the days when donors give to charitable organizations because they say they need it. Lack of funding is not a need. In fact, positioning your organization as being in dire need of money to continue operations weakens your agency. You are branding the organization as one that is desperate—a position of weakness. Your need, in fact, has nothing to do with the nuts and bolts of how your organization operates. The true need your organization is addressing is the community need. It is people going hungry and not being able to function, or youth dropping out of school and not being able to support themselves, or people not being able to get enough drinking water because of a polluted water supply. Your need is about people and communities. It is never about a lack of funding.

Need is also not lack of a program. Programs are organizational structures. If they are to continue, they must sustain themselves. You don't even want to go there. Your need is not about sustaining a program. Your need is about people. It's not your programs that are important—it's the impact your programs are making. What is the issue your organization addresses? How does your organization make people's lives better? That is the need you must talk about. Again, it's not funding or program. It's community need.

One trick I learned early on was to state the need I thought I was meeting and then ask "why?" until I couldn't anymore. For example, one organization I worked with needed funding to bring a home-visiting

The needs your request will meet should focus on people and community. Your reason for existence is to improve the world in some way. The focus of your needs statement, then, should be on issues in your community, not your organization.

practical tip

parenting program to a particular community. Of course, stated that way—with funding and program front and center—I was going to get nowhere. So I started asking myself "why?" Why did I want to implement a home-visiting parenting program in this particular community? Well, it didn't have one, while other communities did. Why was that a problem? Because the child-abuse rates were lower in families that had experienced the home visiting program than among those that had not. So the need I was addressing was high incidences of child abuse. Defining the need this way allowed me to describe all the evils of child abuse and its outcomes. Describing child abuse as the issue means that I could talk about its detrimental emotional, physical and mental affects on the developing child. In addition to all the personal affects which lead to poor health and interpersonal functioning, I could talk about the societal costs of child abuse such as the need for increased medical interventions, runaway and homelessness shelters, and juvenile justice and court systems, to name a few. These are strong statements. Describing program or funding as my need doesn't get me there. Conversations about needing money lead me to justifying organizational finances; describing program needs leads me to justifying my continued existence. Neither of them leads to strong statements about community needs.

Once I've identified the issue and described why it is important to address it, I must also answer the question of *why this particular community?* Does this community have higher rates of substantiated abuse than other communities? Does the community have high concentrations of people who historically have poor parenting skills, such as teen mothers? Does the community have poor public transportation systems where people have trouble getting to where they can congregate in groups, so home visiting makes sense? In other words, why should funders choose to meet the need in this particular community as opposed to others? Answer that question for them.

So it is community needs, not organizational needs, that you must focus on. The needs statement is the crux of your proposal. It helps match your organization's mission to that of the funder. It shows you are aware of the issues affecting your community and that you are a part of the solution. The description of need lays the basis for describing the impact your program makes. It justifies your organization's existence.

How are you going to meet it?

In contrast to the needs statement where your focus is not on your organization, in answering this question, it is. This is the place to talk all about how your program works. In my experience, this is one of the easiest questions to answer because the information is readily available to me from the people who will be implementing the program I describe. This is the collaborative part of grant writing.

The answer to how your organization will meet the described need will tell the funder how much planning and forethought went into developing your program. Program planning is crucial. If you have not planned well, your proposal will fall apart here.

One of the best tools I use to ensure I cover all the bases is a logic model. A logic model is a one-page chart that shows your program's overall goal, its objectives, the activities your organization will engage in to meet the objectives, the resources your organization needs to carry out those activities, how you will measure organizational success in meeting the stated objectives and the time frames in which you will be measuring that success. If a logic model is done correctly, it is easy to see how the different parts of your proposal relate to one another. The logic model becomes the outline on which you base your methodological and evaluative narratives. With an outlined structure in place, it becomes easier to maintain consistency throughout your proposal. Federal grants usually require a logic model be submitted as part of the application.

There are many examples of what logic models can look like. Using the search term "logic model" on the internet will bring up several examples. The format I like, when a format is not prescribed, is shown in the *Sample Logic Model* on the next page, which is just an example of a format. You might have more or fewer objectives depending on the scope or complexity of your program. You might have more or fewer activities designed to meet each objective. You might have some resources that will be used for more than one activity.

Sample Logic Model

Organization
Name
Program Name
Goal:

Objective 1	Activity 1a	Resources for 1a	Objective 1
	Activity 1b	Resources for 1b	measurement and
	Activity 1c	Resources for 1c	timeframe
Objective 2	Activity 2a	Resources for 2a	Objective 2
	Activity 2b	Resources for 2b	measurement and
	Activity 2c	Resources for 2c	timeframe
	Activity 2d	Resources for 2d	
Objective 3	Activity 3a	Resources for 3a	Objective 3
	Activity 3b	Resources for 3b	measurement and
			timeframe

The way I show that my program is making the impact on the community need I have outlined is by carefully crafting my goals and objectives and then measuring progress against them. I need to communicate to the funder that what I'm doing and how I'm doing it have purpose. And my purpose is to carry out my mission. I must show throughout my proposal that I am mission driven.

So how do you come up with good goals and objectives? Well, your goal statement will be the impact you are hoping to make in the community regarding the issue you have described. For example, a goal would be to improve high school graduation rates or reduce teen pregnancy or decrease the incidence of child abuse. The goal statement is broad and global in scope. A good goal statement will directly relate to your community need, the interest area of the potential funder. By focusing on the goal statement, you will better be able to match the missions of you and your potential funder.

Objectives, on the other hand, are specific, measurable and time oriented. For example, your broad goal might be to reduce teen pregnancy. You might have a specific objective to raise the average age of first-time motherhood from seventeen to eighteen years of age within five years. Or you might have a broad goal of improving high school graduation rates. In this case, your specific, measurable and time-oriented objective might be to increase school attendance to 95 percent over the course of a year. In both cases, notice that the goals are very broad while the objectives are specific, measurable and time oriented.

One way that helps me write good objectives is to separate out process from outcomes. Process is about what my organization does. The place to talk about my organization's expertise and success in implementing program is in the proposal's credibility statement. Outcomes are about meeting community needs and making my organization's corner of the world a better place to live. Therefore, to be relevant, the objectives need to measure progress in the community, not how well the organization implements its programs.

Focusing on measurable objectives that are related to the needs you describe keeps your proposal consistent with itself. Your objectives relate to your need through your goal. And, as we shall see, specific, measurable objectives make your evaluation methodology easier to design.

There are many ways to skin a cat, i.e., meet objectives. For example, you can raise the age of first-time motherhood by providing education on pregnancy prevention or by providing contraception. Or you can raise high school graduation rates through a mentoring program with successful graduate role models or an after-school program enhancing study skills. Which one you choose depends on who your organization is, what the organizational values are, what the organization has experience doing and what has been shown to work in the field.

Usually funders do not stipulate the specific activities to be undertaken to reach certain goals and objectives. Governmental and research grants might be a huge exception, however. Many governmental grants, particularly federal ones, are looking to fund organizations that can implement prescribed best practice models. In these cases, your activities are already given to you, and your mission match will not only relate to your goal statement but also to your specific activities.

Notice, though, that in my proposal I do not measure how well I conduct my activities. Instead, I measure how well I meet my objectives. This is a crucial distinction. For example, I can hold as many after-school sessions as I like with as many kids as I like, which are my activities. It doesn't matter how big I am, though, if I don't show an improvement in educational outcomes. I must show funders I am impacting the community need I have described and not spinning my wheels. I need to show results.

Relationships with the people who must implement the methodology you describe and are accountable for the outcomes you promise are critical to the program's success. We will talk about building successful relationships with the key organizational players in Chapter Seven.

How will you know if you are successful?

As we have seen, defining success is related to your objectives, which are outgrowths of your goal, which are stated in terms of your impact on the community need you chose. To write good objectives, then, you have to know what kind of impact you want to have in your community. This impact must be realistic. Funders have a pretty good idea of what realistic means. Through the many proposals they receive, funders get lots of information from many organizations about what success in the field looks like. You must not over-promise or under-promise.

You must have in mind what impact you want to have in the community before you start writing your goal statement. Your program goal, in fact, is the broad statement of how you define success. And the objectives define what program success will look like in specific terms. If your organization is mission driven with a good mission statement, then you will already know how success is defined in the organization. Your program goal will then be a sub-goal of the overall organization and be in line with the overall organizational mission. You will have a program that is consistent with activities elsewhere in the organization, which makes for ease of proposal program implementation and prevents mission drift.

In addition to how well you fulfill community needs, success is also defined by how you stack up against other organizations. Not only must you have thoroughly researched the community needs, to be competitive you must also make sure you have thoroughly researched the standards and practices in your field. Funders receive hundreds of applications, only a few which can be funded. You will be compared to other agencies that meet the same need you do. You need to make sure that you at least meet minimum standards in the field. This is why incorporating best practice models into your program and organizational operations is such a good idea. If you incorporate best practices, you automatically establish some credibility and level of excellence in what you do. Research best practices. Know what works in the field. Use others' success to help you define your own success. Funders will use this benchmark. You should too.

Success

Defining success is an important function of the proposal. When you begin to state your request, you want to talk about what can be... if only you had the funder's support. Let them know what great success they can be a part of.

finition

---

How will you measure that?

In your logic model and thus your proposal, you measure your success by how well you meet your objectives. If you've written specific, measurable time-oriented objectives, defining those measurements is easy. For example, if you want to increase the age of first-time motherhood from seventeen to eighteen in five years, then you know that you need a baseline of age at time of first child today and one at five years. You will also need to measure your incremental progress, that is, your efforts at reaching your goal. So, you might want extremely specific mothers' ages, for example age stated in year with monthly or weekly increments, for every year that you track data. If you are instead trying to raise high school graduation rates, you will need to know how many students begin and end high school today and how many do at the end of your intervention. You can then figure out percentages to see if you've impacted the problem. You will also need to define what measurement standards you are using. For example, is this high school graduation by eighteen years of age or at any age? And how do you define graduation? Is it receiving a high school diploma or an equivalent or either one? Whatever the case, the measurements you use will affect how you both write your objectives and your evaluation of meeting them.

How much will it cost?

This is your budget and specific funding request. Both your budget and your narrative request should state how much your total program will cost, how much money and resources you've raised so far and the amount of funding you are asking from this particular funder. This way, the funder knows if your monetary request fits within its giving preferences, how much its funding will be leveraged and if you will have adequate resources to implement the program in the way you've described.

Before you apply for funding, make sure you will have the resources on hand to deliver on your promises when you say you will. Sometimes there is a huge lag between program implementation and cost reimbursements. You will need the advice of your finance person to see if you can handle the lagging cash flow.

watch out!

You need to make sure you have adequate resources to do what you say you can do. If you don't have adequate resources to implement a promised program, you are setting yourself up for failure. For one thing, without adequate resources your chances of successfully implementing your program are poor. Cutting corners means you will not be able to do all that you promise in the way that you promise to do it. If this is the case, you will not be able to meet all of your legal obligations to the funder should your program be funded. Grants are legal contracts: Funders give you money and you give them the outcomes through the activities you describe in your proposal. If you accept money, you had better make sure you can do what you say you can do.

For another thing, if you don't have adequate resources but implement the program anyway, you are putting your organization's financial viability at risk. For obvious reasons, you don't want to do that. Yet that is often what happens when organizations start chasing money for money's sake. The lure of available money looks good in the short run and might help keep an agency going on a temporary basis. The grants writer looks good because the grant is keeping the agency afloat. But sooner or later, if the agency cannot adequately leverage its resources so it can afford to absorb the total implementation costs associated with running its programs, the agency goes broke. The agency might die a slow death, but usually that is after it has veered from its mission and started focusing instead on activities associated with available funding. The agency then needs to re-define itself since it cannot fulfill the promises in its original mission. Then you have a whole host of governance and branding issues that are beyond the scope of this book. For further information on governance and branding, see the resource list in *Appendix C.*

Do you have community support?

Showing community support is vital to your efforts in pursuing funding. Community support leverages your resources, including a funder's contribution. It gives your organization context and speaks to the necessity of its existence as an important community resource. It boosts your organization's credibility and reputation. It shows that your organization and its members are contributors in meeting community needs and solving community problems. Community support is crucial to developing and maintaining success.

All nonprofits, no matter how new or small, can show some kind of community support, if only through their board members' affiliations and activities within the community.

practical tip

There are many ways your proposal can show it has community support. Your budget and funding request, if done as stated above, will show how many resources are coming from organizations other than the funder, i.e., direct community support. A representation of community members on your board reflects direct community input and support. Any data gathered by or from the community for needs assessments, program designs or program evaluations shows direct community support and buy-in. Any program goals or objectives in line with stated community plans also shows community buy-in to meet the needs you've described. Accepted best practices imply community support.

You want to be explicit in how you are involved in community partnerships. For example, what associations are your organization members of? What meetings do various people in your organization participate in? Did your organization have input into public forums such as hearings, focus groups or planning committees? Direct partnerships scream community support. Do you hold meetings, workshops or conferences open to the public in public places? Do you share resources with or receive in-kind contributions from another community agency? Does your organization have an agreement or memorandum of understanding with any other entities? What contracts has your agency entered into, and with whom?

You also need to be explicit as to how community members are involved with you. For example, how many members of the public have accessed your services? How many people volunteer for your organization? Are members of your organization called upon by public representatives for input or services? Do other community agencies rely on your agency's continuum of services to complement their own? Do professional association agencies look to members of your organization for expertise?

> It took me a while to catch how easy this is. I couldn't see the forest for the trees. The nonprofits I have worked for engage in the these types of activities on a regular basis—it was an expected part of us doing business. Showing strong community support was just a matter of me putting in writing what we already do.

How will you sustain your efforts?

Funders do not want to attract leeches, that is, organizations that cling to them for survival. They don't want to be the sole resource organizations depend on for long periods of time. As such, most funders give funding for a limited amount of time, usually one year. They not only want to know how their contribution will be leveraged, they also want to know what you're going to do once their contribution runs out. In other words, how will you sustain your efforts over the long haul?

Since their contribution will hopefully be a financial one, the obvious arena to address sustainability is in finance. Again, we go back to planning.

What is your plan for raising funds for your program? Do you need initial seed money as an original investment in what will eventually be a self-supporting program? How is the program going to fund itself? How long will it take to do that? What steps do you need to take to get there? If the program will not become self-supporting, what other kinds of fundraising efforts are in place? Do you have a specific fundraising plan? What is it? How much money do you expect to generate each year by following it? If grant development is a major part of that plan, what type of research have you done regarding other and future funders? Who are your prospects? Remember, funders are a relatively small group who are aware of and rub shoulders with one another. They know who the players are in their area of interest. Showing that you have that same awareness shows that you have done your homework and are prepared. Planning in general shows that you have done your homework and are prepared. Come across that way— you will be seen in a much more positive light for it.

There are more subtle ways to address sustainability as well. A history of many years shows that your organization knows how to manage its programs and position itself for survival through various economic and political climates. It also shows leadership capabilities that will help sustain the organization into the future. A history of expansion shows that your organization has the skills necessary to acquire resources and manage growth. Strong community support shows that the organization has the relationship-building skills necessary to leverage resources and meet public need. Sustainability, then, is an important component woven throughout your proposal.

What makes your organization uniquely qualified to do what you propose?

This question is really a marketing question. Put in those terms, the question is really asking what your unique marketing position is. The answer to this question will tell funders why you think you are the best choice out there among the many they have to choose from. You need to differentiate your organization from your competition and come out at the head of the pack.

To differentiate your organization and your program, in Chapter Three we talked about the importance of highlighting your strengths and addressing your weaknesses. This is the time to do that. To get a leg up and get closer to the head of the pack, you want to be seen as simpatico with the funder. In Chapter One we talked about the importance of researching funder communications and co-opting their language and format cues. In Chapter Two we talked about the importance of understanding funder perspectives and how that information can help you present information to various funders.

My foray into marketing and marketing concepts barely scratches the surface. I heartily endorse further study into these concepts. I have listed some resources to get you started in *Appendix C*.

As we have discussed, there are other more subtle ways to set your organization apart from the pack. One is to contact the funder before proposal submission. Another is to follow all the funder's guidelines. Still another is to submit your proposal before deadline. Match missions. Be neat. Leave lots of white space. Tailor each proposal you write. Proofread. Make sure there are no typos. Make sure your budget numbers match up. Make sure all the parts of your proposal are consistent with one another. These are simple rules, yet ones not followed by many organizations. Take plenty of time in your planning and execution. The results will be worth it.

If you answer the above eight questions in every proposal you write, you're going to be in good shape.

To Recap

In your needs statement, talk about community rather than organizational needs.

Develop a logic model to guide your methodology.

Define and measure success.

Leverage your efforts through wide community support.

Make sure your finances are adequately leveraged.

Address sustainability.

Create a unique marketing position statement.

Chapter Five

Crafting Your Budget

IN THIS CHAPTER

···→ Determining your personnel expenses

···→ Dealing with fringe benefits

···→ Stating your revenues

···→ Developing your budget justification

D eveloping the budget is probably the most vexing task of all for new grants writers. Perhaps for experienced grants writers too. In every class and every workshop I have ever conducted for students, the most perplexing part of the proposal has been about developing the budget.

Take heart. I am a successful grants writer but am not a numbers person. I need help too. The good news is that you can develop your budgets in conjunction with other members of the staff. In Chapter Seven we will address working with program and finance staff.

Note that your budget is a financial representation of your proposal narrative. If it's in your narrative, it needs to be in your budget. And if it's necessary to your budget, it should be explained in your narrative.

Determining Expenses

In developing my budgets, the first thing I do is to determine expenses. I have to know how much my program is going to cost in order to raise enough revenue for it. The trick in developing good expense budgets is making sure to include ALL your costs.

Personnel Expenses

Personnel expenses are those that involve paying the organization's employees. Note that these are expenses relating only to full and part time employees, not consultants. Consultants are not employees; they are classified differently by the IRS. They are not on payroll. They pay taxes differently than employees and are not eligible for fringe benefits. Expenses relating to consultants are included in a different section of your budget. If you have questions about whether someone in your organization is classified as an employee or consultant, ask your accounting people.

Many organizations operate more than one program and/or have many different funding sources. Staff responsibilities might encompass more than one program. Thus a particular person's work time might be allocated to two or more programs or funders. The organization might also operate a large program requiring more than one staff to engage in the same activity. The way to account for partial or more than one employee is by calculating a position's full time equivalency, or FTE.

FTE's measure how much payroll it takes to fulfill certain jobs within an agency. One FTE equals one full-time person. Therefore, if a person only spends half time in one job or is only allocated half time to that funding source, you would describe that in your budget as a 50 percent FTE. In the same vein, if you have two staff members doing the same job in the same program allocated to the same funding source, that would be described as two FTE's.

The way to come up with how much expense that particular job requires is to multiply the FTE by the salary for that position. For example, if you have a 50 percent FTE being paid $30,000 per year, the personnel expense is $15,000. If, on the other hand, you have two FTE's being paid $28,000 each, that personnel expense would be $56,000. Your personnel lines, then, might look something like this:

Sample Personnel Budget Lines	
Program Director	$15,000
(50% FTE @ $30,000/year)	
Program Coordinator	$56,000
(2 FTE's @ $28,000/year)	

Fringe Benefits

Fringe benefits are those things that the company pays for as part of its compensation package but are not direct wages. Health insurance, disability insurance and social security are a few common fringe benefits. There are two ways to show fringe benefits.

The first is as a percentage of salary. If fringe benefits cost the company 30 percent of a person's salary, the fringe benefit rate would be 30 percent. Fringe is calculated on the total of all the personnel lines, rather than separately. For example, your personnel budget including fringe benefits might look something like this:

Sample Personnel Budget with Fringe Rate	
Personnel	
Program Director	$15,000
(50% FTE @ $30,000/year)	
Program Coordinator	$56,000
(2 FTE's @ $28,000/year)	
	$71,000
Fringe @ 30%	$21,300
TOTAL PERSONNEL	$92,300

Most funders accept this way of showing fringe and you will be using it in most of your budgets.

The second way to show fringe is by spelling out each fringe benefit separately. This is required for all federal grants. The personnel portion of your budget in this case might look something like this:

Sample Federal Personnel Budget

Personnel

Program Director	$15,000
(50% FTE @ $30,000/year)	
Program Coordinator	$56,000
(2 FTE's @ $28,000/year)	
	$71,000

Fringe Benefits

F.I.C.A. @ 7.65%	$5,432
SUI/DIS @ 2.30%	$1,633
Workers Comp @ 2%	$1,420
Health Ins @ 15.74%	$11,175
Disability @ 0.31%	$220
Pension @ 2%	$1,420
	$21,300

There might be more or fewer line items depending on the benefits your company includes in your compensation package. The above percentages will also vary depending on your state's mandatory contributions, your organization's health insurance costs and your company's contribution toward your retirement plan. Your finance people will have accurate fringe breakdowns.

Non-personnel Expenses

Non-personnel expenses are all the non-payroll costs associated with your operating program. Non-personnel expenses include such things as client assistance, educational materials, client transportation, rent, utilities, computer equipment, office supplies, postage, conferences and trainings, staff travel, classified advertising, employee medicals, etc. Your exact line items and their associated costs will vary according to the needs of your program and your organization.

A non-personnel budget might look like this:

Sample Non-personnel Budget	
Non-personnel	
Direct Assistance to Clients	$3,500
Educational Materials	$500
(100 client workbooks @ $5)	
Client Transportation Vouchers	$500
(100 vouchers @ $5)	
Consultant	$800
Rent	$14,400
($1,200/month for 12 months)	
Utilities	$2,400
($200/month for 12 months)	
Computer	$800
Printer	$200
Office Supplies	$500
Postage	$100
Staff trainings	$750
Staff travel	$250
Classified advertising	$150
Employee medicals	$150
(2 @ $75)	
	$25,000

The best people to guide you on what line items and where to find costs are your program people, who know how much of what the program uses, and your finance people, who are aware of the organizational needs and costs, such as rent. We talk more about coordinating proposal budgets with program and finance staff in Chapter Seven.

General and Administrative Expenses

General and administrative expenses (G&A) are the overhead or general operating expenses of an organization. G&A includes things

Sample Expense Budget with G&A

Expenses

Personnel

Program Director	$15,000
(50% FTE @ $30,000/year)	
Program Coordinator	$56,000
(2 FTE's @ $28,000/year)	
	$71,000
Fringe @ 30%	$21,300
Total Personnel	$92,300

Non-personnel

Direct Assistance to Clients	$3,500
Educational Materials	$500
(100 client workbooks @ $5)	
Client Transportation Vouchers	$500
(100 vouchers @ $5)	
Consultant	$800
Rent	$14,400
($1,200/month for 12 months)	
Utilities	$2,400
($200/month for 12 months)	
Computer	$800
Printer	$200
Office Supplies	$500
Postage	$100
Staff trainings	$750
Staff travel	$250
Classified advertising	$150
Employee medicals	$150
(2 @ $75)	
Total Non-personnel	$25,000

Total Personnel	$92,300
Total Non-personnel	$25,000
	$117,300
G&A (10%)	$11,730
TOTAL EXPENSES	**$129,030**

such as executive director, human resources, and finance staff salaries, organizational audits, and overall agency marketing materials such as annual reports or newsletters. G&A are costs associated with the functioning of the organization as a whole rather than a specific program.

An expense budget that includes G&A might look like the sample on the page to the left.

G&A is generally calculated as a percentage of personnel and non-personnel costs. General and administrative expense percentages vary widely between different organizations in different fields. You should research and be familiar with rates of other organizations like yours so that you know how you stack up and can justify any large deviations from the average.

Sometimes an agency is so small that its program expenses *are* the agency expenses. If that is the case, then you will not have any G&A on your budget as all the organizational costs will be included as your program costs.

Sometimes general operating expenses are not allowed by the funder. If that is the case, do not include a G&A line in your budget. Be aware, however, that you will still need to somehow cover these costs. A common way for nonprofits to leverage their grant funding is by engaging in other fundraising activities.

In federal grants, you are never allowed a G&A line. Overhead costs must be allocated specifically to the grant or not included at all. You must calculate the percentage of time every staff member devotes to fulfilling the activities described in the grant. For example, you would add to your personnel costs the portion of your executive director and accounting staff that are allocated to that grant.

Federal grants have prescribed categories in which to put your expenses as well. In a federal grant, then, your expense budget might look like the *Sample Federal Expense Budget* on the following two pages.

Notice that I added 5 percent of the executive director's time and 10 percent of the accountant's time. You might have more or fewer personnel line items depending on who your general administrative staff are and how much of their time is devoted to carrying out the activities associated with this particular grant. Your numbers will vary, too, according to the salary structure in your agency.

Sample Federal Expense Budget

Personnel

Executive Director	$5,000
(5% FTE @ $100,000/year)	
Program Director	$15,000
(50% FTE @ $30,000/year)	
Program Coordinator	$56,000
(2 FTE's @ $28,000/year)	
Accountant	$4,000
(10% FTE @ $40,000/year)	
	$80,000

Fringe Benefits

F.I.C.A. @ 7.65%	$6,120
SUI/DIS @ 2.30%	$1,840
Workers Comp @ 2.00%	$1,600
Health Ins @ 15.74%	$12,592
Disability @ 0.31%	$248
Pension @ 2.00%	$1,600
	$24,000

Supplies

Office Supplies	$500
	$500

Other

Direct Assistance to Clients	$3,500
Educational Materials	$500
(100 client workbooks @ $5)	
Client Transportation Vouchers	$500
(100 vouchers @ $5)	
Consultant	$800
Rent	$14,400
($1,200/months for 12 months)	
Utilities	$2,400
($200/months for 12 months)	

Sample Federal Expense Budget (Cont'd)	
Computer	$800
Printer	$200
Postage	$100
Staff trainings	$750
Staff travel	$250
Classified advertising	$150
Employee medicals	$150
(2 @ $75)	
	$24,500
Total Personnel	$80,000
Total Fringe	$24,000
Total Supplies	$500
Total Other	$24,500
TOTAL EXPENSES	**$129,000**

Sometimes in federal grants you have a negotiated indirect cost rate in lieu of general administrative expenses. If that is the case, you do not incorporate any overhead costs into your budget. Instead you use the predetermined indirect cost rate. Indirect cost rates are negotiated with the federal government apart from program budgets. If you are interested in an agency indirect-cost rate, you will need to contact the federal financial representative listed in the NOFA or funding announcement.

Sample Revenue Budget	
Revenues	
Funding Source A	$47,900
Funding Source B	$25,000
Funding Source C	$15,000
Funding Source D	$14,400
Funder from which you are requesting funds	$15,000
Your agency	$11,730
TOTAL REVENUES	**$129,030**

Stating Revenues

Most funders want to see their funds leveraged with other funders. They want to see the commitment of the requesting organization as well as other community players. In other words, they want to see if the people who say they support you put their money where their mouth is. Your revenue budget will show that.

Your total revenues should equal your total expenses. You want to show that the funder's contribution is needed for your program's success. You also want to show that you are requesting enough resources that your program will be financially viable. And you want to show that your request does not exceed what is needed. In other words, you want your budget to show the funder what its contribution can do.

In-kind Contributions

In-kind contributions are the non-monetary donations that support your program. For example, if another community organization allows you to use its space for your program at no charge, that is an in-kind contribution. You can have many, many different kinds of in-kind contributions. It can be food, supplies, furniture, equipment, trainings, and so on. In-kind contributions can also include volunteer time. There might be many non-monetary resources contributing to the success of your program.

There are IRS requirements for accepting and receipting donations of any kind, monetary and non-monetary. Although accounting for donations is a function of the finance staff, you should be familiar with the guidelines in your role as a resource developer. You will be the one interacting with the funder. You will be the one who thanks the donor for the contribution. And you will be the one responsible to justify your budget to the funder.

practical tip

In-kind contributions, although non-monetary in nature, do have a monetary value. The value of an in-kind contribution is the amount you would have to pay for it if it wasn't being donated. For example, how much in rent would you have to pay if you didn't have that donated space? Or how much is that equipment worth that you don't have to buy? You need to be careful and not overestimate how much your in-kind contributions are worth. You need to be honest and maintain integrity.

The value of some in-kind contributions are dictated by law, including volunteer time. If you have a professional donating professional services that already have a value, then you are allowed to use that rate. However, if volunteers are functioning in any other than their professional capacities, there is a prescribed rate of how much monetary value you can claim. Make sure you check the applicable IRS literature for all of the rules regarding volunteer time and the most current allowable rates for valuing it. The IRS also has strict guidelines in valuing donated property, most notably vehicles. If you are going to accept used vehicles, be familiar with IRS guidelines.

In-kind contributions will be listed in the revenue lines as a financial contribution from whomever is providing the resource. The value of that contribution will also be listed in your expense budget, but as a cost line item. The two will cancel each other out. The source of the contribution will be described in your proposal narrative and your budget justification.

A revenue and expense budget that includes in-kind space might look like this:

Sample Revenue and Expense Budget	
Revenues	
Funding Source A	$47,900
Funding Source B	$25,000
Funding Source C	$15,000
Funding Source D	$14,400
Funder from which you are requesting funds	$15,000
Your agency	$11,730
Total Revenues	$129,030
Expenses	
Personnel	
Program Director	$15,000
(50% FTE @ $30,000/year)	
Program Coordinator	$56,000
(2 FTE's @ $28,000/year)	
	$71,000
Fringe @ 30%	$21,300
Total Personnel	$92,300

Sample Revenue and Expense Budget (Cont'd)	
Non-personnel	
Direct Assistance to Clients	$3,500
Educational Materials	$500
(100 client workbooks @ $5)	
Client Transportation Vouchers	$500
(100 vouchers @ $5)	
Consultant	$800
Rent	$14,400
($1,200/month for 12 months)	
Utilities	$2,400
($200/months for 12 months)	
Computer	$800
Printer	$200
Office Supplies	$500
Postage	$100
Staff trainings	$750
Staff travel	$250
Classified advertising	$150
Employee medicals	$150
(2 @ $75)	
Total Non-personnel	*$25,000*
Total Personnel	*$92,300*
	$117,300
G&A (10%)	$11,730
TOTAL EXPENSES	**$129,030**

Notice that this budget shows broad community support. It shows that the potential contribution is critical to the success of the program. Revenues equal expenses, which demonstrates the program's financial viability.

In this example, I have in mind two in-kind contributions. Funding Source D's contribution is valued at the same amount as rent. Your agency is contributing the same amount as G&A costs. The explanation that these are in-kind as opposed to cash contributions will be explained in your proposal narrative and budget justification.

Matching Requirements

Many times, particularly in government grants, funders have matching requirements. This is usually expressed in the funding notice as a percentage of total budget. For example, if a funder requires a 25 percent match, a total budget of $100,000 would require that your organization provide $25,000 of that budget. If the funder was offering $100,000 of funding, however, your total budget will figure out to be $133,334; $25,000 is only 20 percent of a total $125,000 budget. You need a 25 percent match. If you're like me, you will have to ask a finance person to calculate match amounts for you.

A match may be in cash or in-kind. Cash is usually preferred. Having a cash match does not necessarily mean that your agency needs to make that contribution. Cash donations from other funders count as cash match. A required cash match does not preclude in-kind donations either. You can have both. You just need to make it clear in your proposal narrative and budget justification who is donating what.

A federal budget requiring a cash match might look like the one below. In this example, I have only calculated the expense portion of the budget, as the sources of revenues are already identified in the match columns. In this example, the funding source has $100,000 available and requires a minimum 25 percent cash or in-kind match. To request the full amount of available funding, then, my total budget will have to equal at least $133,334 and my match must equal at least $33,334.

Sample Federal Expense Budget with Match					
	Federal Share	My Agency	Donor A	Donor B	Total
Personnel					
Executive Director	-	$5,000	-	-	$5,000
(5% FTE @ $100,000/year)					
Program Director	$15,000	-	-	-	$15,000
(50% FTE @ $30,000/year)					
Program Coordinator	$56,000	-	-	-	$56,000
(2 FTE's @ $28,000/year)					
Accountant	-	$4,000	-	-	$4,000
(10% FTE @ $40,000/year)					
	$71,000	$9,000			$80,000

Sample Federal Expense Budget with Match (Cont'd)

Fringe Benefits

F.I.C.A. @ 7.65%	$5,432	$688	-	-	$6,120
SUI/DIS @ 2.30%	$1,633	$207	-	-	$1,840
Workers Comp @ 2.00%	$1,420	$180	-	-	$1,600
Health Ins @ 15.74%	$11,175	$1,417	-	-	$12,592
Disability @ 0.31%	$220	$28	-	-	$248
Pension @ 2.00%	$1,420	$180	-	-	$1,600
	$21,300	$2,700			$24,000

Supplies

Office Supplies	-	$1,500	$2,500		$4,000
		$1,500	$2,500		$4,000

Other

Direct Assistance to Clients	$3,500	-	-	-	$3,500
Educational Materials	$1,500	-	-	-	$1,500
(100 client workbooks @ $15)					
Client Transportation	$500	-	-	-	$500
Vouchers					
(100 vouchers @ $5)					
Consultant	$500	$300			$800
Rent	-	-	-	$14,400	$14,400
($1,200/months for 12 months)					
Utilities	-	-	-	$2,400	$2,400
($200/months for 12 months)					
Computer	$800	-	-	-	$800
Printer	$200	-	-	-	$200
Postage	-	$150	-	-	$150
Staff trainings	$700	-	-	-	$700
Staff travel	-	$250	-	-	$250
Classified advertising	-	$150	-	-	$150
Employee medicals	-	$150	-	-	$150
(2 @ $75)					
	$7,700	$1,000	-	$16,800	$25,500

Sample Federal Expense Budget with Match (Cont'd)				
Total Personnel	$71,000	$9,000	-	-	$80,000
Total Fringe	$21,300	$2,700	-	-	$24,000
Total Supplies	-	$1,500	$2,500	-	$4,000
Total Other	$7,700	$1,000	-	$16,800	$25,500
TOTAL EXPENSES	$100,000	$14,200	$2,500	$16,800	$133,500

In this budget you can see that I have community support, I have asked for the maximum amount of funding allowed and I have provided adequate match. My Agency matches various personnel, fringe, supplies and other line items. Match from Donor A is $2,500 in the office supply line and Donor B is $16,800 for rent and utilities. These line items will be more fully described in my proposal narrative and budget justification.

Notice in this example that I ask for $4,000 in office supplies. My intent is to ask for $1,500 in consumable office supplies (pens, pencils, paper, staples, etc.) and $2,500 in office furniture. The reason that I put the office furniture under supplies is that federal guidelines stipulate that office costs less than $5,000 be put in the supply line.

The Budget Justification

Most grants do not require a budget justification and you will not need to provide one. In all cases, however, every revenue and expense you list in your budget must be mentioned in your proposal narrative. Your budget must contain no surprises. Everything in your budget must come from your narrative and everything in your narrative must be reflected in your budget.

Larger grants, though, most notably federal grants, require budget justifications. A budget justification is simply a line-item narrative explanation of how your costs were derived. Budget justifications show exactly the same information as the budget. While budgets are financial statements expressed in monetary terms, budget justifications are narrative statements explaining those monetary terms.

An example of a budget justification for our previous federal budget would look something like the following:

Sample Federal Budget Justification

Personnel
Executive Director. The executive director will spend approximately 5 percent of his time in activities associated with this grant at a salary of $100,000 per year. My Agency will contribute the $5,000.

Program Director. The program director will spend half her time in activities related to this grant at a salary of $30,000 per year. Federal share is $15,000.

Program Coordinator. Two full time program coordinators are needed to implement the program as described in this grant. A Program Coordinator's salary is $28,000 per year. The $56,000 will come from Federal share.

Accountant. The accountant will spend 10 percent of her time in activities associated with this grant at a salary of $40,000 per year. My Agency will contribute the $4,000.

Fringe Benefits
F.I.C.A. F.I.C.A. is calculated at @ 7.65 percent of salary. Federal share is $5,482 and my agency share is $688 for a total of $6,120.

SUI/DIS. Unemployment benefits are calculated at 2.30 percent of salary. Federal share is $1,633 and My Agency share is $207 for a total of $1,840.

Workers Comp. Worker's Compensation is calculated at 2 percent of salary. Federal share is $1,420 and My Agency share is $180 for a total of $1,600.

Health Ins. Health benefits are calculated at 15.74 percent of salary. Federal share is $11,175 and My Agency share is $1,417 for a total of $12,592.

Disability. Disability insurance is calculated at 0.31 percent of salary. Federal share is $220 and My Agency share is $28 for a total of $248.

Pension. Retirement plan contributions are calculated at 2 percent of salary. Federal share is $1,420 and My Agency share is $180 for a total of $1,600.

Sample Federal Budget Justification (Cont'd)

Supplies
<u>Office Supplies</u>. Consumable office supplies such as pens, pencils, paper, staples and such are estimated to be $1,500 per year to be contributed by My Agency. Donor A is contributing office furniture worth $2,500 to the program. Total costs for office supplies is $4,000.

Other
<u>Direct Assistance to Clients</u>. The program will provide direct assistance to clients such as emergency food and clothing. Federal share is $3,500.

<u>Educational Materials</u>. Program participants will be required to have workbooks as part of their educational training. We estimate serving 100 clients. Each workbook cost $15. Federal share is $1,500.

<u>Client Transportation Vouchers</u>. Vouchers for clients to travel to and from the program site where trainings are help is estimated to be $500. Federal share is $500.

<u>Consultant</u>. A consultant will be hired to help design and implement an evaluation study at $80 an hour for 10 hours. Federal share is $500 and My Agency share is $300 for a total cost of $800.

<u>Rent</u>. Rent for program office space is $1,200 per month for 12 months for a total of $14,400. Office space will be donated by Donor B.

<u>Utilities</u>. Utilities are estimated to average $200 per month for 12 months for a total of $2,400. Utilities are being donated by Donor B.

<u>Computer</u>. The program will need to purchase one computer. Computers cost an average of $800. Federal share is $800.

<u>Printer</u>. The program will need to purchase one printer. Printers cost an average of $200. Federal share is $200.

<u>Postage</u>. The program will require additional mailings including program newsletters, meeting announcements and updates. We are estimating

---

Sample Federal Budget Justification (Cont'd)

program mailing expenses of $150 per year. Postage costs will be contributed by My Agency.

Staff trainings. The program coordinators are required to undergo a three day certification training. Cost for the trainings are $350 each for a total of $700.

Staff travel. Program coordinators will be reimbursed 45 cents per mile for travel to and from clients' homes and the required trainings. Two program coordinators are budgeted for 312 miles each for a total of $250. My Agency will be contributing the $250.

Classified advertising. Classified advertising to recruit program coordinators will cost $150. My Agency will contribute the $150.

Employee medicals. Two program coordinators will need to hired and undergo agency medical examinations. Medical exams are $75 each. My Agency will be contributing the $150.

Notice that in the budget justification each line item's cost derivation is explained in detail in the order it appears on the budget.

practical
tip

To Recap

◆ Outline your expenses first.

◆ Make sure to include ALL of your expenses.

◆ Have revenues equal expenses.

◆ When stating revenues, include in-kind contributions.

◆ Show the monetary value of in-kind matches.

◆ Be detailed in your budget justification.

Chapter Six

Writing the Proposal

IN THIS CHAPTER

···→ Formatting your proposal

···→ The default format

···→ The writing process

···→ Attachments

We now turn our attention to the mechanics of actually writing the proposal. The most important thing to remember in formatting the proposal is to always follow the lead of the funder. You also need to answer the eight questions every funder wants answered that we discussed in Chapter Four, whether the funder explicitly asks them or not.

Presentation of Information

You want to thoroughly review any application guidelines so that you know what information the funders are looking for. If they give an outline of how they want the material presented, follow it. If they ask questions, put your information under those headings and order the headings in the order they ask the questions. If they give evaluation criteria, make sure you answer those questions. Always follow the rules of the funder. Know those rules. Know what they're looking for. Do your research.

I always start writing out my proposals using an outline of the funders' formats. Using that outline, I see where any evaluative criteria they have asked for would fit. Then I go through the eight questions and see where those answers fit into the outline. This way, I ensure that: 1) funders can easily find the information they are looking for in my proposal; 2) I have answered all the questions they have asked of me; and 3) I have submitted a proposal that will address ALL their concerns, whether explicitly asked or not.

Remember, ALWAYS follow the rules of the funder.

Default Format

If the funder doesn't give you any clues as to the order of information it prefers, I use the format listed below.

1. Cover letter

2. Executive summary

3. Background and credibility statement

4. Needs statement

5. Goals and objectives

6. Methodology

7. Evaluation

8. The Request

9. Sustainability

10. Budget

11. Budget justification

Although this is the default presentation I use when I have no formatting clues, this is not the order in which I write it. We will talk about the order in which to write each section after we outline the default presentation format.

Cover Letter

The cover letter is a brief one- to three- paragraph document written in letter form to the funder contact. It summarizes what is included in the proposal package. It also summarizes each section of the proposal, usually in one or two sentences for each section. Make sure that in summarizing your financial information, you state the total cost of your program, how much you have raised so far and how much you are asking from the funder.

Background and Credibility Statement

This section introduces your agency to the funder. The background and credibility section is where you define what makes you uniquely qualified to do what you're proposing to do. This is where you state your mission and give background on your organization. You will also talk about any community partnership you have. We talked about how to brand your organization in Chapters One and Two, how to best present your agency to funders in Chapter Three and how to present community support in Chapter Four.

If I have a specific program for which I am writing, I will only spend a paragraph or two talking about my overall organization. The bulk of my background material will be about the specific program I am looking to fund.

Needs Statement

The needs statement is the crux of your proposal. It is community needs that drive your organization's mission and community needs that spur the funder to give. Your needs section must be solid. Remember, need is never lack of a program or lack of funding. Need is about the community.

Need can be substantiated in many different ways. Statistics documenting poor or unacceptable outcomes are common. Trend statistics, or those that track a problem over time, are very helpful in foreshadowing an initial baseline for program evaluation. Use statistics from respected sources in the field. Government studies, published research, expert statements—all are used.

Funders from urban southern California might be reading your proposal from rural Minnesota. They might not know much about your community. Your job, then, is to paint a picture of what your community looks like, the issues your community grapples with and the impact the un-met need you are describing has on your community's residents. Use data to tell people how large your geographic community is and how densely populated it is. State the average age of your residents. Funders might also want to know things like employment rates and average income. If ethnicity is relevant, describe the ethnic population of your community.

If you are talking about the need for affordable housing, you will also need data about homelessness, rent expenses and rental availability. If you are talking about a health issue, you will need disease data. If you are talking about at-risk youth, you will need child welfare and educational data. The list goes on and on. In short, in addition to painting a picture of the community your organization operates in, paint a picture of the population your organization serves. What issues do the people you support grapple with? How many people are affected by them? How do the issues your organization impacts affect the health and well-being of those you serve?

Then talk about the services at your community's disposal, how accessing them works, any waiting lists they have, any barriers to services such as language or disability, culture or psychological impediment. Talk about the gaps in the services that exist, and why. Lay the foundation for why you're doing what you're doing in the way that you do it.

The needs assessment takes up a significant portion of the proposal, as it should. Your community needs are the front and center of your program. In a five page proposal, my needs assessment is usually at least three quarters of a page long.

practical tip

This is also where you want to highlight any best practices you are proposing. You want to talk about the impact they have made on other communities and how you think they can impact yours.

A multitude of community-level data can be accessed through the census bureau. Descriptive data can also be found on local and state websites. Chambers of commerce can give you a landscape of the business community. Professional associations generally

publish a wealth of
information relating
to their specialty
areas. And, of course
governmental agencies
and departments
collect loads of
information that is
available to the public.

A lot of research goes into developing a
thorough needs statement. Well written
needs statements contain a lot of information
yet are extremely concise. Don't let concise
sentences fool you—it takes a long time to
completely research all your facts.

Goals and Objectives

Your goal is a broad statement of the impact you hope to make on the need
you described in the needs assessment. My goal statement usually begins
with an infinitive verb, is one sentence long and labeled "Goal." In a longer
grant, I might have more than one goal, in which case I still have single
sentences but label them "Goal 1," "Goal 2" and so on.

Objectives are specific, measurable and time oriented. They state the
precise ways you are going to achieve your goal. My objectives begin with
root verbs. They are usually bulleted sentences placed under the goal they
relate to. My goals and objectives are the shortest part of my proposal.
A goals and objectives section might look like the *Sample Goals and
Objectives* on the following page.

Notice my goal is a broad statement about the impact I want to make in
my community. My objectives, on the other hand, are extremely specific,
measurable and time oriented. Well-written objectives lead to easy
evaluation.

My goals and objectives, along with my methodology and evaluation, come
from my logic model. We discussed logic models in Chapter Four.

Methodology

The methodology describes how your program operates both within the
community and as part of your organization. Methodology describes
the processes and procedures you are implementing in order to meet
your objectives. The methodology section is usually a longer section, just
because describing all that process can be laborious.

One way that I use to understand what my program processes and
procedures are is to think of a program participant's travels through my

---

Sample Goals and Objectives

Goal: To reduce the incidence of child abuse in Somerset County.

Objectives:

◆ Teach 25 parents with developmental disabilities appropriate child development and behavior as measured by pre- and post-testing.

◆ Teach 25 parents with developmental disabilities positive behavioral support techniques as measured by pre- and post-observation sessions.

◆ Teach 25 parents with developmental disabilities appropriate anger management techniques as measured through pre- and post-observation sessions.

◆ Have no reports of child abuse and neglect among program participants during and six months following training.

---

program—from finding the program to permanently exiting the program. Questions I want to answer here include:

❑ What mechanisms does my organization have in place so that people can find us? How will my program be marketed?

❑ How do people access our services? What are my intake processes?

❑ How are people assessed for services? Are there intake criteria?

❑ What happens once people are accepted into our program? How long before they receive services? Are there waiting lists?

❑ Where is the program activity being held? How do people get there? What makes it accessible to the community?

❑ What exactly are the specific interventions? How will they be implemented? How long will they last?

❑ Are there incentives for people to complete the program? What are they?

❑ How do people exit the program? Are there exit criteria? How are people readied for exit from the program?

❑ Does the organization provide follow-up services? How do people access those? How are they terminated?

❑ How does the organization keep track of clients? What is the record-keeping system?

❑ What kind of information do we collect? What does my organization do with that information?

❑ How does my organization deal with confidentiality issues?

❑ What processes are in place to evaluate client progress?

❑ What processes are in place to evaluate program success?

❑ What staff are involved in implementing the program? What are their job descriptions? What are their qualifications?

In longer grants, funders might want to know about organizational procedures too. I have been asked about agency recruitment and retention efforts, agency supervisory systems, staff evaluation, accounting procedures, quality assurance systems, other fundraising activities, management information and technology systems and agency data storage and protection. Be prepared.

Evaluation

When you evaluate the impact of your program, you evaluate how well your program is meeting its objectives as opposed to how well the program implements its activities. If you have well written objectives, your evaluation statements will be easy. Developing good goals and objectives was covered in Chapter Four.

Since my evaluation statements measure my progress toward my objectives, my evaluation statements mirror my objectives. Both are a bulleted list of short sentences and are presented in the same order. That's it. The tools and processes I use to measure my results are outlined in my methodology; I don't need to reiterate them. All that's left to do is articulate the results I hope to achieve.

Using the sample objectives previously listed, a sample evaluation section might look like this:

Sample Evaluation

At the end of the program period:

◆ Twenty-five parents with developmental disabilities will show they have learned a significant amount of appropriate child development and behavior as measured by pre- and post-testing.

◆ Twenty-five parents with developmental disabilities will demonstrate positive behavioral support techniques as measured by pre- and post observation sessions.

◆ Twenty-five parents with developmental disabilities will have learned appropriate anger management techniques as measured through pre- and post-observation sessions.

◆ Have no reports of child abuse and neglect among program participants during and six months following training.

The Request

This section of your proposal is probably going to be the shortest, one paragraph long. Your request simply states your total program costs, the amount of funding you've raised so far and from whom, and the amount of the request.

A sample request might look like this:

Sample Request

Implementing the XYZ Program at My Organization will cost $100,000. Funds raised so far total $72,500, with another $10,000 pending. To date, My Agency has secured contributions from Donor A in the amount of $25,000 and Donor B in the amount of $15,000. Donor C will be providing office space and furniture valued at $20,000. A request to Donor D in the amount of $10,000 is pending. My Agency is contributing $12,500 to the project. We are requesting that Funder ABC contribute $17,500 to help prevent child abuse and neglect in Any County.

Sustainability

This section is also very short, usually two paragraphs or so. This section outlines what efforts your agency has in place to continue its current activities and sustain its financial viability. We discussed how to do this in Chapter Four.

Budget and Budget Justification

We talked about developing budgets and budget justifications in Chapter Five.

Writing Format

I have given you a guide for what to include in your written default proposal. I *write* the sections, however, in the following order.

1. Goal

2. Needs statement

3. Objectives and methodology

4. Evaluation

5. Budget

6. Budget justification

7. The request

8. Sustainability

9. Background and credibility statement

10. Executive summary

11. Cover letter

I have found that writing the proposal in this order helps me to ensure that the proposal is consistent with itself.

My first task is to match my program's goal to the funder's goal. This helps me keep my focus on the funder's priorities. I then formulate a broad goal statement.

I next identify the need I want to impact and thoroughly research it. I also research my community. This step helps me focus on community needs as opposed to program needs.

Third, I create a logic model where I formulate objectives and methodology. I then write my objectives under my goal statement, followed by writing out my methodology.

My next step is to state the results I hope to achieve. I parallel my results with my objectives.

My fifth step is to develop my budget and budget justification. That way, I know how much revenue I need to successfully implement my program before I make the ask.

I make my request once I am sure I can procure all the necessary resources to implement the program in the way that I describe in the proposal and maintain organizational financial viability.

Then I address how the organization will sustain the program.

Not until now do I have all the information I need to write a comprehensive background statement and answer the question of why my organization is uniquely qualified to do what I propose. I now do that.

If an executive summary is required, I do it last. Instead of trying to fit my proposal into the format of my summary, I use the summary to give an overview of what is contained in my proposal.

Once the proposal package is assembled, I write the cover letter.

Remember that you need to format the information according to the rules of the funder. I do that by rearranging the information into the formatting outline I have previously created. We discussed how to develop that outline in the beginning of this chapter.

Attachments

Almost all proposals require attachments. If you are going to be writing a significant number of proposals throughout the year, it is a good idea to have the most common attachments always on file. This file is commonly referred to as an evergreen file.

First and foremost, your evergreen file must contain your IRS determination letter. Funders are constantly asking for proof of the 501(c)(3) status of those seeking funding from them. If you don't have ready access to one or can't find your organization's determination letter, contact the IRS for an updated copy of this documentation. And make plenty of copies.

The next two documents are financial ones: your organization's audit and your organization's 990. Funders want to know their contributions will be managed well, that your organization is a good steward of their finances. Your organization's audit and 990 are good indicators for funders. Sometimes funders ask for two or three years' worth of financials; a good evergreen file will have financials going back three years. Your finance people will have all the statements you need.

You also need human resource information such as an organizational chart, job descriptions and resumes. Of course, you might not have an organizational chart or job descriptions for new programs and positions you are seeking funding for. If this is the case, make sure you leave yourself plenty of time to formulate them.

For federal grants, you will also need a DUNS number. A DUNS number is a numerical code that Dun and Bradstreet gives to your organization when you register with it. They are free to get and they are required to submit a grant through grants.gov. If you are going to submit a federal grant, make sure that you leave plenty of time to get your DUNS number and register your organization with grants. gov.

I have missed deadlines before because I did not adequately anticipate how long it would take me to assemble a complete submission. In addition to your main proposal, make sure you leave plenty of time to assemble attachments and make copies.

You are now ready to copy and submit your proposal. Before submission, check

 Confession!

your work carefully. Let someone else proofread what you have put together. You don't want to be knocked out of the competition because your proposal is lacking something, is not consistent within itself or comes across as sloppy. Pay attention to details.

To Recap

◆ When formatting your proposal, follow the lead of the funder.

◆ Write your needs statement first. It is the crux of your proposal.

◆ Articulate your goal to match the funder's.

◆ Take care in preparing your logic model. It is the basis of your methodology and evaluation.

◆ Formulate your request after you develop your budget.

◆ Address how you will sustain your efforts.

◆ Answer the question of why you think your organization is uniquely qualified to do what you propose.

◆ Write your summary materials last.

◆ Create an evergreen file.

Chapter Seven

Developing Success: It's a Team Effort

IN THIS CHAPTER

··· ➜ Including program implementers in program planning

··· ➜ Describing executive director and board roles

··· ➜ Acquiring information from human resource and finance personnel

··· ➜ Interacting with marketing personnel

S uccess doesn't just happen—you must work for it and develop it. Early in my career they told me that the basis of strong proposal writing is strong program planning. My experience has taught me this is true. Good planning, hence good proposal writing, is not done in a vacuum. It is not solely you raising money—it is an organizational effort. Your successes and failures affect the whole organization. It is only fair that others develop and share in your success. You must establish effective relationships and gather input from all levels of expertise in your organization.

Engaging Program Personnel

The most obvious people to talk to are your program people, those implementing the processes and procedures you describe. They are the ones who have to meet the proposal's objectives. They have to live within the funder's restrictions. And they have to give you the reporting data. It is not enough just to receive the funding. You will have to show that your organization can deliver on your promises. You must make sure BEFORE the proposal is submitted that the people responsible for delivering on your promises know what's in store for them should you get funded.

This is not always easy since program people are extremely busy. In these times of scarce jobs and shrinking government resources, they are probably trying to meet a huge increase in demand for services with no corresponding increase in resources. In fact, in many organizations, resources have shrunk and there have been hiring freezes or reduced hours or even layoffs. Program people must do more with less. They feel more stress. Morale might be down. They might question their effectiveness as waiting lists grow longer and people are turned away. They might feel that no matter how hard they work, they never seem to make a dent in the need they see. Program people are on the front lines. They are the people who have to deal with a multitude of challenges on a very personal level. They might be a little preoccupied.

It is important to understand that you might represent additional workload that isn't immediately relevant to their daily tasks. Developing budgets, gathering resumes and creating job descriptions pales in comparison to finding someone a place to live or dealing with a program participant's current crisis. And if you obtain funding, that means even more demands to deal with, such as new objectives to fulfill, funding restrictions to deal with and reports to compile. Even if you have a great relationship with the program staff, you still need to be aware of how your requests affect their daily tasking.

So what do you do? In my experience, it is YOUR responsibility to work with THEIR schedules, not their responsibility to work with yours. If you know they are harried, ask them when a good time to meet is. Give them plenty of time. Ask them how long it will take them to get back to you. Develop task deadlines *with* them, not for them. And thank them continually for getting things to you when they said they would. Let them know how much their efforts are worth. Letting them know the results they are a part of achieving will help them establish their priorities and will allow them to appreciate the results of their efforts.

Let them know that the only reason you can even ask for funding is because they are doing their jobs well. They are the ones on the front lines. Let them know

Employees, like donors, want to part of something bigger than themselves. If the program you describe in your proposal is in line with the organization's mission, values and vision and everyone is on the same page, you will encounter almost no resistance. This, however, only occurs if you have done your homework and your proposal is in line with organizational objectives.

 practical tip

that if they weren't doing their jobs, you wouldn't have anything to write about. It is because they are successful that you are successful. It is not about you raising money, it's about them raising money by doing their jobs.

Treat your program people as you would any donor—make them a part of something bigger than themselves and thank, thank, thank and thank again! Think of your co-workers as crucial in-kind contributors to your fundraising efforts. Make them feel a part of your team. Help them feel like they are a crucial part of a system bigger than themselves.

Describing Organizational Leadership

Everybody wants to please the boss. Everyone knows they have to get along with their boss to keep their job. That's a given. If you don't get along with your boss or if you think your boss is a jerk, you might need outside advice in order to effectively continue in your work environment. But what in the world does this have to do with proposal writing? Well, just as with program personnel, there are things that you will need from the top leadership in order to be successful. You need to be on a positive footing with the organization's leaders.

Let's start with the easy things first. You're going to need a list of your board directors. Sometimes funders ask how often boards meet, so a schedule of board meetings is also good to have on hand. Sometimes funders ask for board governance policies; get those too. Know how the board straddles the line between governance of the organization and management of the organization. Sooner or later you will be asked this. Know how the board defines success, how it evaluates itself and how it evaluates the executive director. In today's environment, you also want to know how it determines executive compensation. (See how quickly the questions can become probing?)

The board is ultimately responsible for the health and viability of the organization. It defines the mission. Stick to the mission. If you see that the organization is experiencing mission drift, you have a responsibility to let your executive director know. DON'T complain directly to board members. It is your executive director's job to make sure that the organization is carrying out the vision the board. If the executive director is not on point, then you want to talk to him or her, not his or her bosses. If the board is not on point, then it is the executive director's job to work with them and let board members know what their suggestions mean for organizational functioning. Even if you work directly with the board, go to the executive director first.

The board is also responsible for determining the vision of the organization. This is done in concert with the executive director. Most often the board's vision, and strategy for getting there, is articulated through a strategic plan. In my opinion, strategic planning is crucial to developing the success of an organization. Program planning should not take place in a vacuum. Make sure you have a copy of your agency's strategic plan and that you are familiar with it. Every individual program plan, hence any proposal, that you write should fit into the goals and objectives of the organization's overall strategic plan.

Some funding is not worth pursuing. If

Strategic plans are great tools to have on hand. Strategic plans state in concrete terms the activities the organization will take to implement its vision in accordance with its values. Strategic plans should contain information on the strengths and weaknesses of the organization. They should also include an external environmental assessment outlining the threats and opportunities in all the markets in which the organization operates. If done thoroughly, they will also have the input of key organizational players including board, staff, consumers, donors, legislators, business representatives, other community agencies and members of the public.

practical
tip

your proposal's program plan does not support your agency's strategic plan, don't apply for the funding. Number one, you do not want to be responsible for mission drift. And secondly, you want to appear well managed. One of the ways you establish your organization as having good management is to show that every part of your agency is on the same page. The strategic plan gives everyone the same road map on how the organization will achieve success. Stick to the road map. If the funding is not going to get you where the organization wants to go, don't apply. Instead, spend your time researching and competing for funding that will help your agency implement the vision that everyone is striving toward.

Engaging the Management Team

I am constantly asked by funders about my organization's leadership team and what qualifications it has to manage the organization. (Maybe not in the smaller foundation grants, but almost always in the corporate grants and always in the governmental grants.) As a grants writer, the first thing you need is all the team's resumes and job descriptions. In addition, I am also often asked for brief biographical sketches of each executive team member. To save time, I keep a paragraph or so of this information on hand. For specific programs, you might also need the additional resumes and job descriptions of all staff positions outlined in your proposal. Make sure this information is accessible too. But generally you need biographies only for the executive management team.

The executive director is THE executive leader of the organization. Executive director leadership affects how the organization is managed and perceived. In doing the biography of the executive director, concentrate on your organization's brand and what image you want to present. Think especially about corporate relationships and the importance they place on the CEO position. Remember all those questions we asked in Chapter Two about success and viability that corporations will be interested in? Well, the executive director is the steward for all of this. Make sure your sketch of the executive director states how he or she has achieved success, makes reference to his or her financial acumen and talks about his or her management skills. That way, you can use the executive director biographical sketch for both proposal writing and marketing purposes.

Next to the executive director, the director of human resources is crucial in maintaining organizational operations. If your organization is big enough, this might be a chief of operations or associate executive director position.

Make sure your executive director and senior management team have current resumes. They are a great tool in compiling your biographical sketches. Of course, you have to remember to update them yearly. Take the initiative in making sure you have the updated information you need. For example, as part of my annual planning process, I make sure resumes and bio's are updated to include any new initiatives the agency has undergone over the past year that would include them.

 practical tip

If your organization is not that big, this person might also be your executive director.

Staff is usually the biggest expense within any organization, whether for-profit or nonprofit. It takes people to provide services to other people. Human resources people know your recruitment policies and procedures. It knows your turnover rate. It knows your recruitment strategies. It knows exactly how many full and part time staff the organization employs. It has resumes and job descriptions. It has organizational charts. It knows what benefits are offered to employees and how the benefits plan compares to other nonprofits in your field. Human resources has a wealth of information that funders, particularly government funders, ask for.

Be familiar with human resource policies and procedures, as you will need to be able to explain them to funders. Funders, especially governmental funders, often ask for staffing information beyond the resume and job description.

 practical tip

Of equal importance is your director of finance. If you are a smaller organization, this role might be fulfilled by your executive director or even a board member. And monitoring specific program budgets might be the responsibility of a program director or even you, if you are a grants manager and have responsibilities for grant budget oversight.

Finance people are a wealth of information. They have your organization's IRS determination letter, overall organizational budget, audits, 990's and charitable registration certificates. Sooner or later, you will need these documents.

You need the finance people to help you set up your annual fundraising plan. The finance people will know what is adequately funded and what is underfunded. They can give you a sense of financial priorities for the organization, which can guide your program planning and the type of money you are looking for. They can tell you about cash flow and whether the agency can afford to implement a program on a reimbursement basis. They will know whether the agency accounting systems can handle a funder's reporting requirements.

Finance people are also crucial in helping you develop your individual proposals' budgets. They have your organization's payroll information. They know how whether a person is classified as exempt or non-exempt. They know exactly how many hours a person puts in. They know how much the consultants cost. They know your organization's fringe rate, that is, what percentage of salary benefits, such a health insurance, cost. They can give an exact breakdown of each benefit the agency offers, which you especially need for federal grants. Finance people know what your general operating expenses, or overhead, are. They know the line-item breakdown of your overhead, which, again, you'll need in many proposal budgets. They track the costs of every expense of every program in your organization. They can help you project what line items you will need to cover all program costs.

Finance people are not only important in developing budgets, they are important to helping you understand things such as interpreting financial statements and audits. Trust me, some day you will be in front of a funder justifying your request and you will be asked about the organization's finances and why things are the way they are. You want to have your finance people's perspective BEFORE that happens.

> I have always worked closely with the finance people in every organization I have worked for. A practice I have found particularly helpful is to run my budgets by both the finance and program managers to make sure that they both can live within the budget I'm submitting should we be funded.

practical tip

If you think program people aren't very familiar with what you do, human resource and finance people are even more removed. They can't always respond to you on your timeline. For example, if it is end-of-the-month reconciliation time or the auditors have just arrived, your finance person is not going to be able to respond to your last-minute request. If an employee just got hurt on the job, your human resource person has a more immediate concern than your request for an organizational chart. It is crucial, and I say that with emphasis, that you get your ducks lined up in a row way before you see a deadline on the horizon. You need to be prepared. Proper planning not only prevents poor performance but can also lead to mutually-satisfying working relationships.

Just as with the program staff, you need to allow for emergencies and setbacks not only with your job, but also with theirs. You need to respect their time and their schedules. If you need something with a quick turnaround in order to submit a timely proposal, ask them how you can help them meet that deadline. Don't wait until the last minute. That way, when emergencies on your part do come up, it will be seen as an unforeseen aberration and, consequently, other people will be more willing to interrupt their day to get you what you need.

Preparing in advance has another huge advantage—it means your proposals, most often, will be in before deadline. That's a huge thing—it puts you way ahead of the pack as most proposals are received at deadline. Plus, getting things in early positively builds your brand. Your organization will be seen as being prepared and well-managed, a nice edge to a well-written proposal.

practical tip

If you really want to make your management team members feel good about assisting you, show them how they are part of your success. At team meetings, let everyone know how important that employee handbook or organizational budget was to your request that got funded. Thank, thank, and thank them again for doing their jobs so well. You wouldn't be able to do what you need to do without them. Celebrate your successes with them. Let them see how what they do on a daily basis is part of that success. Make them feel like you make your donors feel—a part of something bigger than themselves. Help them see how important their contributions are.

Interacting with Marketing and Public Affairs Staff

In smaller organizations, you might be all the fundraising, marketing and public affairs staff there is. In larger organizations, there might be a slew of other fundraisers and another whole department of marketing and public affairs staff. In either case, it is important that your proposal-writing efforts complement your agency's related activities.

As stated previously, you don't chase funding just for funding's sake or just because it's out there. You must coordinate your efforts with your organization's priorities, which should be more than just get money. A strong organization is about mission, not money. If you are an enthusiastic fundraiser doing his or her best to raise money, remember why you are doing it. It's hard to do this if day in and day out you experience constant pressure to enhance the financial bottom line. But always put mission first and foremost. It is mission that motivates, not money. As I stated in the Introduction, no one has ever funded me because I needed the money.

Revenue generation is not an end in and of itself—it is a means to an end. The end is the difference your organization is making in its corner of the world. And revenue generation is but one method of many in achieving that difference.

Marketing and public affairs are closely related to proposal writing. All three specialties deal with the public. All three require promotion of the agency's brand. All three influence public perception of the agency.

In writing proposals, your public is foundations, corporations and government representatives. You put forth a product, a mission and a goal, and try and sell them to your public, the funders. You have an edge if your organization has a positive reputation, or brand. If you have marketing staff, their job is to create and protect the organizational brand. They have insights into the needs of the public and can measure public perception. Marketing staff can help you understand and contribute to maintaining your organization's brand. They can also help you understand your organization's strengths and weaknesses in the marketplace.

Public affairs staff deal with legislators. You do too. You must understand the political environment in which your organization operates. Public affairs staff will have that insight. They will know what issues and legislation are on the horizon that will affect governmental funding streams. They will also be aware of legislation affecting the governmental oversight of nonprofits in general. You want to be aware of these things so that you are prepared to answer questions from funders. They are nonprofits too. They know what's going on in the political environment that might affect their grantees. Show you are prepared for any environmental threats your organization might face and will survive them. Show them you are well managed. Be prepared. Let public affairs staff help you.

> I have never worked for an organization large enough to have its own fundraising, marketing and public affairs departments. As a result, I have found it extremely beneficial to allocate some of my professional education opportunities to topics in these specialties. The breadth of skills I acquired has vastly improved my ability to develop proposals and get them funded.

 Confession!

Building positive working relationships with other members of the organization is crucial to your success as a grants writer. Achieving success is a collaborative effort. Since program staff are responsible to meet your proposal's promises, they should be part of the planning process. Human resource staff can help you with the workplace processes and procedures you need to include in your grants. Finance people are responsible for our organization's financial viability as well as fulfilling program financial reporting requirements. They should also be consulted before promises are made. Proposal writing activities are closely related to and intertwined with organizational marketing and public affairs activities. To achieve maximum success, make sure to get the input of marketing and public affairs staff. It is a team effort. Everyone on the team must work together if the organization is to thrive and you are to succeed in raising money.

To Recap

◆ Always include program personnel in your proposal planning.

◆ Help program and administrative staff see how important their contributions are.

◆ Be able to articulate both governance and management practices.

◆ Avoid mission drift.

◆ Build close relationships with human resource and finance people.

◆ Align your grant writing activities with marketing and public affairs efforts.

Chapter Eight

People Give to People: How Do You Stack Up?

IN THIS CHAPTER

···→ The usefulness of personality inventory

···→ Exploring natural abilities

···→ The importance of healthy self-esteem

···→ Putting it all together

If you want to help positively brand your organization, you need to build your own personal brand. You need to know what you're all about and feel comfortable in your own skin. Why is this important to proposal writing? Because people give to people. More accurately, people give to people they trust. Often, you are the only person from your organization with whom a potential funder interacts. You become the face of the organization. If you are perceived positively, your organization might or might not be funded. However, if you are not perceived positively, your organization will probably not be funded.

Increased self-awareness leads to better work performance. Better work performance leads to positive personal and organizational brands. A positive brand helps develop to success.

Using Personality Inventory

I am lucky enough to have had a multitude of opportunities for self-exploration over the years. One of the tools I have found helpful in understanding myself is the Myers-Briggs Type Indicator. The Myers-Briggs measures personality characteristics and is useful in understanding where your energy comes from, how you receive and process information, your decision-making styles and your preferred work environment.

The theory of personality types was first postulated in 1921 by Swiss psychiatrist Carl Jung in his book "Psychological Types." Intrigued by his theories, Isabel Myers-Briggs and Katherine Cook Briggs, her mother, wanted to take Jung's ideas and make them more understandable to the common person. They believed that Jung's psychological types could be a useful, everyday life tool. So during World War II, the two women developed the Myers-Briggs Type Indicator personality inventory. In the 1990's, Meyers-Briggs results were correlated to career options and the inventory began to be widely used in career counseling.

The Myers-Briggs Type Indicator groups people into distinct personality types utilizing four distinct continuums: introversion-extroversion, sensing-intuitive, thinking-feeling, and judging-perceiving. There are sixteen personality types that are based on which pole a person falls closest to along each continuum. Myers-Briggs attributes personality differences between people within the same category to the differences in where they fall along each continuum.

What in the world does this have to do with proposal writing? Well, lots. Are you an introvert or an extrovert? Do you work better with the big picture or are you a more details person? Do you think more in terms of concepts and ideas or do you relate more in terms of feelings and emotions? Do you come to your decisions quickly and stick to your guns or do you prefer as much information as possible and wait awhile? Knowing the answers to questions like these will help you perform better.

For example, if you are an introvert, you get your energy from being alone and engaging in solitary tasks. Site visits by funders might exhaust you.

If this is the case, the site visit will go much better if you schedule your time so that immediately before and immediately after the visit, you can be alone for awhile. Perhaps you can manage the former by going through the visit in your mind's eye and the latter by writing up a report on the visit. During the visit, you might prefer one-on-one as opposed to a group meeting. Structure the visit, then, so you have lots of one-on-one interaction. You will feel more at ease and be more comfortable in answering the funder's questions.

If, however, you are an extrovert, you get your energy from other people. You might want, then, to have lunch with your buddies and talk about what's going to happen before the visit. During the visit, you might want to schedule a meeting with as many of the players as possible so you can feed off one another. And after the funder leaves, you might want to give your supervisor an oral report before going back and writing it up.

> Along the introversion-extroversion continuum, I test right in the middle, with a slight preference for introversion. This means that I need both time alone and time with other people. To work with these preferences, I plan a variety of both more solitary tasks, such as researching funders or actually writing the proposal, and more interactive tasks, such as planning with others or entertaining funders, in my day. Whenever I have a day of all writing, for example, or a day of all meetings, I am exhausted. It is important for me to maintain balance.

 **Confession!**

Introversion-extroversion is just one of the Myers-Briggs continuums. Knowing where you fall on the other three continuums can be just as useful. For more information about the Myers-Briggs Type Indicator, I refer you to the Myers-Briggs Foundation website at http://www.myersbriggs. org.

Utilizing Natural Abilities

In 1922, a General Electric employee in Massachusetts, Johnson O'Conner, theorized that if people were engaging in tasks natural to their abilities, work efficiency would improve and employees would be more satisfied, thus increasing work productivity and thereby reducing overall company production costs. O'Connor decided to analyze various job tasks to see if he could identify the natural abilities behind them. He developed a series of tests requiring the test taker to perform a number of hands-on tasks. Eventually the laboratory tests were converted to a paper and pencil version. In 1992, The Highlands Company acquired the rights to use the paper and pencil test and called it The Highlands Ability Battery. In 1999, The Highlands Company developed a CD version of the abilities battery and in 2004 an online version.

The Highlands Abilities Battery consists of nineteen different, hands-on work samples, each assessing and defining a natural ability. Abilities are distinct from skills. Skills are acquired over time. Abilities are innate and remain constant throughout a lifetime. By measuring and defining your natural abilities, you will learn not only what you do best but how you can apply what you do best to your work.

So how does this work in a proposal writing context?

Let me give you a concrete example. Two of the abilities that The Highlands Abilities Battery tests for are Concept Organization and Classification. Different scores in these two abilities point to how people prefer to solve problems. Concept Organization is the ability to organize information in a linear, logical way. People who are high in Concept Organization are very analytical. They are the planners of the world. They also tend to be good communicators as they can organize ideas in a way that makes them understandable to others. Classification is almost the opposite problem-solving style. People high in Classification take in information from many sources and pull together strands of thoughts, facts and ideas into a solution without following a linear train of logic. They find pure logic to be limiting and slow. People high in Classification place a premium on action and enjoy fast-paced environments with a lot happening at once. A person can be high in both Classification and Concept Organization, low in both or high in one and low in another. Differences in these combinations point to different strengths and weaknesses, communication styles and preferences in the work environment.

I test extremely high in Concept Organization and extremely low in Classification. I find it easy to plan and prioritize—perfect for engaging in program development. I can also arrange ideas in a logical manner in a way that others can easily understand—perfect for writing proposals. However, I feel a lot of stress in an environment that requires rapid-fire decision-making. Dealing with last-minute, unplanned stuff drives me nuts. I am not the ideal responder to late breaking news or advocacy opportunities. Although I have taught myself to deal with these things and have acquired some skill in dealing with last-minute issues, a lot of last-minute stuff works against my natural abilities. To help me deal with such circumstances, I partner with somebody else who enjoys this type of work. I also take some time out and plan out how I'm going to deal with last-minute demands, thereby utilizing my strong ability in Concept Organization.

I currently work with a team member who likes the rapid-fire environment I abhor. He and I have similar responsibilities in terms of some of the grants that we need to bring in. At first, this caused conflict because of our extremely dissimilar work styles. We soon found out, however, that our differences in styles actually made us a stronger work team. So we now formulate agreed-upon goals, divvy up the workload according to which tasks better fit our work styles and remain in constant communication with one another. This approach has helped tremendously in achieving success.

Let me give you another example. Idea Productivity is another of my natural abilities. Idea Productivity measures the rate at which thoughts run through your mind—not the creativity or quality of those ideas, just the rate of them. What this means is that I have a whole lot of thoughts about a whole lot of things that need to be sorted, evaluated and expressed. It's a very good ability to have for writing and speaking. But I am so high in idea productivity, it is easy for me to take my thoughts and run with them without input from others. I have had to learn how to funnel my thoughts through other people so that they can be included in program development and implementation.

My high idea productivity also points to my need for variety and challenge. I do not do well doing the same thing every day, even throughout one day. Knowing this helps me again plan my work days and weeks. I do best when I have several projects in different specialty areas to work on. And I

> Being strong or weak in one ability or another does not mean good or bad. There are strengths and weaknesses at every level of each ability we have. The trick is in matching what you do well to your everyday work tasks and environment so that you feel more satisfied and fulfilled and so that you can better perform. Working with, rather than against, your natural abilities leads to better individual as well as organizational success.
>
> 👍 **practical tip**

need to partner with those members of my team who do enjoy doing one thing and doing it well. They keep me on point.

The Highlands Abilities Battery tests for nineteen different abilities. Knowing your natural abilities helps you to understand your strengths and weaknesses, thus helping you shape the way you carry out your work and balance what you find fulfilling with what you find stressful.

For more information about The Highlands Abilities Battery, please go to http://www.highlandsco.com.

Improving Your Self-Esteem

Self-esteem is the way we perceive ourselves. It affects how we interpret events around us, the way we present ourselves and how we deal with other people. It permeates everything we do. Any work you do in understanding and improving your self-esteem will have a big pay-off.

People with a healthy self-esteem show tolerance and respect for others, have integrity, take responsibility for their actions and can handle criticism. They take pride in their accomplishments and are self-motivated. They seek the challenge of meeting worthwhile goals, are willing to take risks and are not afraid of failure. They are in command and control of their lives.

When you are asking other people for money, you need to exude confidence, one way to communicate that you can be trusted. People give to other people. If you have a healthy self-esteem, that is, you believe in yourself and your abilities, you will find it easier for others to believe in you too.

It starts with taking the challenge of meeting a worthwhile goal, i.e., meeting your organization's mission. You take a risk and make the ask, not knowing if you will succeed or fail. You need to have a pretty good self-esteem to handle the rejection you will face. You need to know that a "no" from a donor says much more about the donor, the donor's values and the donor's situation, than it does about you. That's why it's important to spend so much time researching and building relationships with your donors, so you know their values and their situation—so you lessen the "noes" that you hear. But no matter how good your research or how good

> I am considered a very successful fundraiser. Last year, I was awarded more than $2.4 million to my agency. However, I was rejected far more than I was approved: I submitted more than $6 million in requests.

 **Confession!**

the relationship is, you will still hear "no" more often than you want. You must be able to handle rejection if you are going to last as a fundraiser. A high self-esteem helps tremendously.

So what can you do to build a healthy self-esteem? Well, that is beyond the scope of this book. There are thousands of books out there about how to improve self-esteem. In addition, maintaining adequate social support systems, like strong relationships with family and friends, is very important. Talking over your fears and failures with someone like a minister or rabbi can help. Sometimes therapy is the answer; there are tons of techniques clinical therapists use to help people raise their self-esteem. Sometimes, becoming more aware of our personality characteristics and natural abilities and understanding how they affect our work environment and relations with other people helps us to more appreciate our individual strengths and understand the conflict in us we sometimes feel. It really doesn't matter what method you choose. Any improvement in self-esteem will help you.

Building Your Personal Brand

The most important characteristic any fundraiser can have is integrity. Exhibiting integrity is crucial to building trust. And building trust is crucial to developing a strong brand. You need to maintain integrity to yourself, to your funders and to your organization's mission and values.

Maintaining integrity to yourself means knowing yourself—your strengths and weaknesses, your abilities and your values—and acting consistently in accordance with them. You need to be honest in presenting who you are. People who know themselves and are secure in that knowledge exude strength. Other people feel secure with them and trust them. They have strong personal brands.

Maintaining integrity with your funders means you are honest with them. If you tell donors that their contribution is to be used for one purpose, then that is the purpose for which the funding is used. Your needs assessment contains accurate facts. Your credibility statements can be verified. Your objectives are reasonable within your budget and organizational capacity. You give true evaluation results in your reporting, whether you met all of your objectives or not. You keep the funders informed and let them know immediately if there are any changes to your project as you described it. In other words, you say what you're going to do and do what you said. Your word has meaning. You are trustworthy and reliable.

You must also maintain integrity with your organization's mission and values. You are an agent of the organization and will often be the only representative of the organization that the donor will know. Always be true to the organization's mission. Match—don't change—missions. Avoid mission drift. Conduct yourself in a way that reflects well on your agency. Being honest with funders about why you didn't meet certain objectives doesn't mean you can badmouth others' efforts. In that same vein, building your organization up doesn't mean tearing other organizations down. Always be respectful.

The more you know yourself the more you will be able to play off your strengths and compensate for your weaknesses. The higher your self-esteem, the better you will be able to handle the rejection you will inevitably face. The more integrity you exhibit, the more trusted you will be. The more consistent you can be with yourself in all these areas, the better personal brand you will have.

To Recap

◆ Explore you personality characteristics.

◆ Explore your natural abilities.

◆ Develop a healthy self-esteem.

◆ Maintain integrity.

Conclusion

Wrapping It All Up

Well, we've come to the end of the book. We've talked about the importance of knowing your potential funder and how to research what they say about themselves. We've talked about what they don't tell you and the context in which they make their decisions. We've discussed how to maintain integrity while matching organizational and funder missions. We've covered the importance of branding and how to create a strong organizational brand. We've addressed how to acknowledge organizational weaknesses by playing off organizational strengths. We've talked about budgeting and actually writing the proposal. We've discussed how your success hinges on other members of your team and how to enlist their support. Finally, we've talked about the importance of self-awareness and development of a personal brand to successful proposal writing. We've covered a lot of ground. So where do we go from here?

Keep it simple and keep writing. The most successful grants writers have lots of experience. But they also listen to their funders and meet their funders' needs. They set themselves and their organization apart in the marketplace. They follow all the funder's rules. They plan and get things in ahead of deadline. They tell the truth. They are self-aware. At least, that's been my experience. I am a successful grants writer. I raise about $1 million a year through foundation, corporate and governmental funding. I'm going to stick with what works for me. I hope it works for you, too.

Appendix A—Sample Grant Proposal for Program Support

COVER LETTER

August 14, 2008

Ms. Jane Smith
The Linden Foundation, Inc.
c/o Grants Management Associates
77 Summer Street, 8th Floor
Boston, Massachusetts 02110-1006

Dear Ms. Smith:

Enclosed please find two application packages for Empowering People's Parent Enrichment Program. The mission of our Parent Enrichment Program (PEP) is to reduce the risk of child abuse and neglect among parents at risk of abusing their children. PEP is a program that positively impacts families and children by helping parents understand their children and preparing them for successful parent-child relationships. Through PEP, Empowering People provides families involved with New Jersey's child welfare system, the Department of Children and Families (DCF) and the Division of Developmental Disabilities (DDD) a strong foundation by providing positive support to the parents and children in regards to their economic, health, living and social service needs. The program's focus provides parents with hands on training, interactive classroom exercises and informational lectures.

PEP is partially funded by DCF, DDD and foundation and corporate contributions. Empowering People is asking The Linden Foundation, Inc. to partner with us in providing $12,500 in general operating support to help positively impact parent-child relationships where the parents have a developmental disability or are educationally deprived.

If you have any questions or would like additional information, please feel free to contact me at 888-555-1212, ext. 570 or joppelt@abc123. org.

Thank you for your consideration of our request.

I look forward to hearing from you.

Sincerely,

Joanne Oppelt
Development Director

COVER SHEET

APPLICATION COVER SHEET
send to: The Linden Foundation
c/o Grants Management Associates
100 Main Street
Boston, MA 12345

Date: 8/14/08

Name Of Organization: Empowering People

Address: 9876 Elm Street, Somerville, NJ 01234

Phone: 908-555-1212

Email: info@abc123.org

IRS Tax Identification Number: 12-3456789

CEO/Executive Director: Charles Roberts

Signature of CEO/Executive Director: _____

Contact for this proposal: (if different) Joanne Oppelt

Phone: (if different)   888-555-1212, ext. 570

Email: (if different)   joppelt@abc123.org

Fiscal agent (if applicant is not a 501 (c)3 organization):

Application for (specify amount): $12,500

Total budget of proposed project: $81,907

_____

Please respond briefly, as some readers receive the cover sheet only.
A more detailed description, of up to three pages, should be included
in the narrative:

Brief description of proposed project:

The mission of Empowering People's Parent Enrichment Program (PEP) is to reduce the risk of child abuse and neglect among parents with special needs and who are at-risk of abusing their children. PEP was developed over fifteen years ago to serve parents with developmental disabilities who have been adjudicated by the courts to take parenting classes. The program serves families from Somerset and Hunterdon Counties in New Jersey. PEP provides a range of services and activities including interactive family activities, individualized assessments, in-home supports, personalized needs-based training and parenting classes that successfully promote the stabilization of the family unit.

Please summarize project objectives: (what will be accomplished?)

The objectives of the PEP program are to:

- Teach twenty parents with special needs child age-appropriate behavior as measured by pre- and post-tests and in-home assessments.

- Teach twenty parents with special needs positive approaches to dealing with stress as measured by pre- and post-tests and in home assessments.

- Teach twenty parents with special needs positive approaches to disciplining their child as measured by pre-and post-tests and in-home assessments.

- Have no substantiated reported incidences of child abuse/ neglect among families while enrolled in the program.

- Link twenty low-income families with a parent or child with a special need with needed social resources such as WIC, food stamps, social security, and employment assistance.

- Provide twenty families with basic resources such as emergency utility, clothing, and transportation expenses.

[OVERVIEW OF ORGANIZATION]

Describe current services provided by the organization:

Empowering People is a community-based, human services agency that was founded in 1979 with a $90,000 grant to move twenty adults with disabilities from state institutions and place them successfully in the community. The agency was founded with the mission to provide community access through effective and comprehensive support services for people with disabilities, giving them the opportunity to live independently and to lead normal and productive lives as citizens integrated into the community. Twenty-nine years later, Empowering People continues to provide quality supports to more than 3,500 New Jersey residents with disabilities per year.

At Empowering People we look at the individuals we serve as vital members of our organization and this is how we refer to them. A variety of individualized support services are currently offered to members including parent training, child development education, housing, life skills training and assistance, education, employment assistance, recreation, money management, health maintenance, family planning, personal counseling, crisis intervention and others.

Geographical area served: Somerset and Hunterdon Counties, New Jersey

Year Founded: 1979
Of Paid Staff: (specify f/t and p/t) F/T: 198; P/T: 152
Of Members: 0

[FINANCIAL SUMMARY]
Provide information from the most recent audit or annual financial statement

Last fiscal year (FY) ended date: 12/31/07

Last FY total expenditure: $16,595,470

Last FY total income: $18,610,733

*if operating surplus or loss more than 5 per cent of total income, please comment:

Please note that audited financial figures include Empowering People and Total Property Management activities. Total Property Management is the real estate holding company for Empowering People. Total Property Management activities reflect all real estate transactions performed on behalf of Empowering People. Most of the revenue in excess of expense is due to the activities of Total Property Management.

Operating fund balance at end of last FY (from audit/financial statement): $11,533,039

Current (projected) FY 2008

Operating Budget: $19,553,476

[SOURCES OF SUPPORT—LAST YEAR]

Please list the dollar amount received and percent of your total support for each

Government grants and contracts: $14,746,000

Program fees/sales and third party payments: $1,514,210

Endowment/interest income: $573,669

Other earned income: $2,853,753

Benefits/special events (includes Corporate Sponsors): $70,808

Membership: 0

United Way: $16,672

Contributions—Businesses:

Contributions—Individuals:

Contributions—Foundations, etc.: $78,900

TOTAL: $19,894,452

Reminder:
Please review the guidelines to make sure you have included all information required

PROPOSAL NARRATIVE

Empowering People

Mission. Empowering People's mission is to provide community access through effective and comprehensive support services for people with disabilities, giving them the opportunity to live independently and to lead normal and productive lives as citizens integrated into the community.

Accomplishments and qualifications. Empowering People is a multi-faceted, human services agency that was founded in 1979 with a $90,000 grant to move 20 adults with disabilities from state institutions and place them successfully in the community. Twenty-nine years later, with a budget more than $19.5 million and a staff of over 400, Empowering People continues to provide quality supports to more than 3,500 New Jersey residents with disabilities per year. In 2004, Empowering People was nationally recognized for its efforts in integrating people with developmental disabilities into society as the recipient of the national Community Inclusion Award from the American Association on Intellectual and Developmental Disabilities.

In 1993 Empowering People added the Parent Enrichment Program (PEP) to its array of services offered to people with disabilities. PEP is a program that positively impacts families and children by helping parents understand their children and preparing them for successful parent-child relationships. Through PEP, Empowering People provides families involved with DYFS and DDD a strong foundation by providing positive support to the parents and children in regards to their economic, health, living and social service needs. All families involved in the program are individually assessed to determine their unique needs and service plan. The program's focus provides parents with hands on training, interactive classroom exercises and informational lectures. This is accomplished through individual assessment, weekly parenting classes, and in-home visits.

Since its implementation fifteen years ago, PEP has become well known for successfully working with families in which the parents, children, or both have a developmental disability. The program has been extremely successful in promoting the growth and development of the parents who have participated in it. Through the PEP program, we have seen increased learning through our parenting classes as measured by post-tests and improvement in parenting skills based on our in-home assessments.

Current programs. At Empowering People we look at the individuals we serve as vital members of our organization and this is how we refer to them. A variety of individualized support services are currently offered to members including housing, life skills training and assistance, education, employment training and assistance, recreation, money management, health maintenance, family planning, personal counseling, crisis intervention and others. In 1993 Empowering People added the Parent Enrichment Program (PEP) to its array of services offered to people with disabilities.

Populations served. Parents are referred to the PEP program by the New Jersey Division of Youth and Family Services (DYFS), New Jersey's child protective agency, into PEP for parenting classes because they have abused or are at-risk of abusing their children. PEP serves low-income families with parents or children with special needs. We service a high minority population, reflective of the community around us. Both male and female children and parents are served.

The Parent Enrichment Program

Need. Every child deserves to be and feel loved, safe and secure. The basis for self-esteem is formed in the beginning years of a child's life and reaches far into adulthood. A healthy parent-child relationship is the primary vehicle through which self-esteem and security are transmitted during the earliest and most formative years. Unfortunately, many children in the U.S. today do not receive appropriate parental affection, affirmation and guidance. They do not feel cared for or valued.

According to the U.S. Administration for Children and Families Children's Bureau publication Child Maltreatment 2006, (the latest statistics that are available), approximately 3.3 million referrals were made to child protective agencies across the U.S. Almost 30 percent of investigations resulted in a finding that the child was maltreated— approximately 940,000 cases. Maltreatment includes neglect, physical abuse, sexual abuse, and psychological abuse. More than 62 percent of child victims suffered neglect, 17 percent were physically abused, 9 percent were sexually abused and 7 percent were emotionally abused. An estimated 1,460 child deaths were related to abuse or neglect. Reports show that 79 percent of perpetrators were parents. The vast majority of children were maltreated by one parent, usually the mother.

Children are at most risk when they are young. Data shows that the rate of child victims declines as age increases. Child abuse also crosses gender lines, except sexual abuse, where the rate is approximately four times higher for females than for males. Tragically, children younger than four years of age account for 77 percent of child fatalities due to child abuse; 90 percent of child fatalities were younger than seven years of age. Children who have physical or intellectual disabilities are at higher risk for child abuse and neglect, as are children from families with parents who have disabilities or parents who are educationally deprived. A child who has suffered from abuse/ neglect has a greater risk of social isolation, running away, dropping out of school, repeated abusive situations with peers, substance abuse, emotional trauma, mental illness and premature death.

Target population. The Empowering People curriculum is for use with families with special needs, that is, those who not only struggle with the demands of parenting but also with the frustrations and limitations of a disability. Since its implementation fifteen years ago, PEP has become well known for successfully working with families in which the parents, children, or both have a developmental disability or the parents are educationally disadvantaged. PEP serves low-income families with limited income and resources. The parents we see are mostly single mothers, some with both a cognitive and physical disability. We service a high minority population, reflective of the community around us. Both male and female children and parents are served.

Goals. Parents involved in PEP have demonstrated at-risk behaviors and intellectual deficits that might contribute to neglect and abusive parent-child situations. Studies have shown that children who have suffered from child abuse and/or neglect have a greater risk of social isolation, running away, dropping out of school and increased use of drugs and alcohol, among others. The mission of PEP is to reduce the risk of child abuse and neglect among parents with special needs with the ultimate benefits of stronger families and healthier children.

The objectives of the PEP program are to:

- Teach twenty parents with special needs child age-appropriate behavior as measured by pre- and post-tests and in-home assessments.

- Teach twenty parents with special needs positive approaches to dealing with stress as measured by pre- and post-tests and in home assessments.

- Teach twenty parents with special needs positive approaches to disciplining their child as measured by pre-and post-tests and in-home assessments.

- Have no reported incidences of child abuse/neglect among families while enrolled in the program.

- Link twenty low-income families with a parent or child with a special need with needed social resources such as WIC, food stamps, social security, and employment assistance.

- Provide twenty families with basic resources such as emergency utility, clothing, and transportation expenses.

Empowering People expects that we will have no substantiated reported incidences of child abuse/neglect among the families while enrolled in the program and improved parenting skills once the program is completed. Empowering People believes that in addition to preventing child abuse and neglect, PEP has other benefits. Children who grow up in healthy families are more likely to succeed in school and less likely to engage in delinquent behaviors. They learn to trust, rather than fear, other people. They are not afraid to form bonds. They experience more joy in life. In the long run, these children become better parents themselves.

Time frame. The program cycle is six months. At the six-month mark, PEP staff meets the DYFS caseworker to discuss the family's progress. If the family has attended and participated in the weekly lessons, completed all necessary goals given by the DYFS caseworker, demonstrated an understanding of child-appropriate behaviors, and improved home safety for children involved, a graduation ceremony is held and the family receives a certificate of completion. If it is decided the family is in need of further services, the family is given an extension of an additional six months.

Budget. See attached.

Staffing. PEP program activities are conducted by a Program Counselor and PEP Director. The Program Counselor conducts weekly parenting classes, regular in-home visits and quarterly case conferences with the Division of Youth and Family Services (DYFS). The Program Counselor also facilitates linking the family to any needed social services such as WIC, welfare, unemployment and social security. In addition, the counselor ensures that the child's educational needs are met through meetings between parents and teachers and obtaining tutoring for the child, if needed. The Program Counselor is also responsible for submitting monthly reports to DYFS and program reports as required.

The PEP Director supervises the Program Counselor and ensures program quality through Empowering People's quality control and review system. The Director receives referrals from DYFS, is the initial contact to the family and conducts the initial family assessment. He revises the specialized education curriculum as needed and oversees its implementation. The Director serves as the PEP program liaison to DYFS and submits the quarterly progress reports to them.

Evaluation. All families involved in the program are individually assessed to determine their unique needs and service plan. The program's focus provides parents with hands on training, interactive classroom exercises and informational lectures. This is accomplished through individual assessment, weekly parenting classes, and in-home visits.

PEP utilizes a standardized assessment tool, The Parent Behavioral Checklist, to assess each family's need. Once the initial assessment has been completed, the family is given the opportunity to discuss the results of the evaluation and actively participates in the development of a Parent Habilitation Plan. The Parent Habilitation Plan enables families to identify, develop, and implement individualized goals that focus on reducing their risk of child abuse and neglect in the future. To determine areas of need and assess and monitor the effectiveness of the parenting classes, pre- and post-tests are administered each week. Empowering People staff work cooperatively with DYFS caseworkers, reporting the results of the pre-tests and post-tests to DYFS. It is the DYFS caseworker who determines when a parent is ready for graduation.

<u>Future funding</u>. PEP is partially funded by and the New Jersey Division of Developmental Disabilities, New Jersey Division of Youth and Family Services and partially by foundation and corporate contributions. Since we are the only parenting program serving families in Somerset and Hunterdon counties where the parents have a developmental disability, the state will continue to fund us through DDD. We have also received multi-year funding from the TJX Foundation. We have a Development Director on staff who diligently researches potential funding opportunities and applies to applicable funding sources.

PROGRAM BUDGET

Empowering People
Parent Enrichment Program
2008 Budget

Revenue

NJ Department of Children and Families	$33,809
NJ Division of Developmental Disabilities	$30,598
TJX Foundation	$5,000
Linden Foundation	$12,500
TOTAL REVENUE	**$81,907**

Expenses

Personnel	
PEP Director	$20,500
(50% FTE @ $41,000/year)	
PEP Program Counselor	$31,240
(100% FTE @ $15,50/hr @ 49 hrs/wk)	
	$51,740
Fringe (31.4%)	$16,243
Total Personnel	$67,983

Non-personnel	
Specific Assistance to Clients	$3,000
Educational Materials	$2,000
Travel	$1,475
Total Non-personnel	$6,475
Total Personnel	$67,983
	$74,458
General and Administrative (10%)	$7,449
TOTAL EXPENSES	$81,907

Appendix B—Sample Grant Proposal for Capital Equipment

August 25, 2009

Mr. John Doe
President
Union Foundation
P.O. Box 0000
Warren, New Jersey 10101-1001

Dear Mr. Doe:

Empowering People

Empowering People is a multi-faceted, human services agency that provides support services for people with disabilities. Empowering People was founded in 1979 with a $90,000 grant to move twenty individuals with disabilities out of state institutions and place them successfully into the community. Our mission is to provide community access through effective and comprehensive support services for people with disabilities and at-risk youth, giving them the opportunity to live independently and to lead normal and productive lives as citizens integrated into the community. Empowering People also takes on the challenge of developing affordable housing.

Empowering People provides supports and gives a voice to adults and youth who traditionally have had little support and no voice in society. We help people with housing, life skills training, vocational skills, employment, health maintenance, money management, socialization, education, crisis intervention, civic activities and community support. Empowering People also supports opportunities for advocacy through training in assertiveness, decision-making and civil rights.

We are one of the few agencies in New Jersey that provides such a broad array of support services for people with developmental disabilities and at-risk youth. We are the only agency in Somerset County that provides a complete and comprehensive continuum of care for people with developmental disabilities as well as youth with special needs who are in New Jersey's child welfare system. We provide more all-encompassing residential and support services than any other organization of our kind.

In 2004, Empowering People was chosen to receive the Community Inclusion Award by the American Association on Intellectual and Developmental Disabilities. This national, annual award is given to a culturally responsive organization that has succeeded in fully including people with disabilities in community life.

In 2006 and again in 2009, CARF, an independent, not-for-profit accrediting body, awarded selected programs at Empowering People a three-year accreditation, the highest accreditation possible. Further, Empowering People was commended in its quest for quality programs and services.

In 2007, Empowering People was honored to receive the NJ Community Development Association award for Excellence in Affordable Housing. Empowering People, in a first-in-the-country financing structure, helped four people with disabilities making 30 percent or less of the area median income, purchase their own homes.

At Empowering People, we believe in working with our members' abilities so as to facilitate as much independence and integration into the community as possible. Our goal is that each member be as independent in individual decision-making and ability to live within the community as he or she is able. We offer housing in over 200 scattered sites throughout Somerset County. Support services are available from 24-hour daily care to as little as two hours a week, depending on members' abilities. Training in independent living skills such as basic hygiene, menu planning, basic math, managing finances, reading, cooking, and food shopping is provided to all our members, depending on need. We also recognize the importance of self-advocacy. Empowering People supports opportunities for advocacy through training in assertiveness, decision-making, community integration and civil rights.

Increasing Organizational Capacity

Nearly 3,000 New Jersey residents live in developmental centers at an annual cost of about $225,000 each, or two to three times the average cost of community living. Compare that with the cost for providing community housing for members of Empowering People, which runs just $50,00 to $80,000 annually. New Jersey's seven developmental centers consume 31 percent of the $1.4 billion budget of the Division of Developmental Disabilities while serving less than 8 percent of the population served by the department. When compared with statewide personal income, New Jersey's spending on institutions ranks sixth in the nation while our investment in community living places us 40th.

While the rest of the nation recognizes the benefits of reducing their institutional populations, New Jersey lags far behind the national average. Since 1969, 140 institutions have been closed throughout the nation, yet only two of those were in New Jersey and the state is not one of the 40 states that plan additional closings. Nine states no longer operate large institutions. Of the remainder, nearly half serve an institution population of 375 or fewer (versus 3,000 in New Jersey).

Clearly the numbers support moving people out of institutions. But so does our moral obligation to ensure we are maximizing the ability of each member of society to live fulfilling lives. Community living offers people with disabilities the opportunity to live in their own homes while receiving the supports they need. They contribute to the fabric of society, in many ways financial—buying goods and services and often paying taxes—while building self-esteem. We began Empowering People in 1979 by successfully removing 20 people with developmental disabilities from institutional living and integrating them into the community. Today we assist more than 3,500 individuals with all kinds of disabilities each year, many of whom become outspoken advocates for community living.

One of the problems facing people moving out of institutions is the lack of decent, accessible, affordable housing. At Empowering People, we have two homes in Somerville where we are not at capacity due to our current fire protection system and ensuing limits in zoning. We have the housing already available. With an upgrade in our fire protection system, we can increase our capacity, thus allowing people with disabilities to come out of institutions while reducing the cost of their supports and increasing their independence and self-sufficiency.

The Request

In 2004, the Union Foundation generously allocated $5,000 to Empowering People to help upgrade our computer software and integrate our computer systems. Because of this contribution, along with others, we have been able to increase our operational efficiency and improve communication between the scattered sites and the main office. In 2006, the Foundation granted us $7,500 toward the purchase of two handicapped accessible vans so that members with physical disabilities can be transported to employment, medical and social appointments. In 2008, Union Foundation monies were leveraged with the Hackett Foundation, Hyde and Watson Foundation and EJ Grassmann Trust to purchase a total of nine hygienic shower chairs. Empowering People deeply appreciates the support of the Union Foundation.

Empowering People would like again to partner with the Union Foundation in helping to meet the housing and support needs of people with disabilities. We are asking the Union Foundation to contribute $10,000 towards the upgrading of our fire protection systems at 1234 and 2345 South Main Street in Somerville, NJ. By upgrading our fire protection system, we will be able to increase our capacity to meet the needs of people with disabilities and affordable housing needs.

Broad Funding Base

In addition to the Union Foundation, $22,500 funding has been secured from the Hyde and Watson Foundation and EJ Grassmann

Trust. A funding application has also been prepared for the Catholic Human Services Foundation.

Administrative Expenses

Empowering People's overhead rate is 10 percent and includes rent; office maintenance and furnishings; office equipment; telephone; office expenses such as printing, office supplies, copying and postage; administrative salaries and fringe; professional fees (legal, accounting and consultant); staff training; directors and officers and multi-peril insurance, classified advertisements to fill positions, dues and subscriptions.

For more information, enclosed please find Empowering People's 2007 Annual Report.

If you have any questions or would like additional information, please feel free to contact me at (888) 555-1212, ext. 570 or joppelt@abc123. org.

Thank you for consideration of this request.

I look forward to hearing from you.

Sincerely,

Joanne Oppelt
Development Director

PROGRAM BUDGET

Empowering People 2009 Fire Protection System Upgrades	
Revenue	
Hyde and Watson Foundation	$15,000
E.J. Grassman Trust	$7,500
Catholic Human Services Foundation	$10,000
Union Foundation	$10,000
Empowering People	$8,100
TOTAL REVENUE	**$50,600**
Expenses	
1234 South Main Street Fire System Upgrade	$25,300
2345 South Main Street Fire System Upgrade	$25,300
TOTAL EXPENSES	**$50,600**

Appendix C—Recommended Resources

For Funder Research

The Foundation Center
http://www.foundationcenter.org

Grantstation
http://www.grantstation.com

GuideStar
http://www.guidestar.org

The Federal Register
http://www.federalregister.gov

Grants.gov
http://www.grants.gov

CD Publications
http://www.cdpublications.com

For Needs Data

US Census Bureau
http://www.census.gov

City Data
http://www.city-data.com

For Federal Budgets

Office of Management and Budget Circulars
http://www.whithouse.gov/omb/grants_circulars

Professional Organizations

CharityChannel
http://charitychannel.com

Grant Professionals Association
http://www.grantprofessionals.org

Association of Fundraising Professionals
http://www.afp.org

American Marketing Association
http://www.marketingpower.com

National Council of Nonprofits
http://www.councilofnonprofits.org

Professional Publications

CharityChannel:
http://charitychannel.com

The Chronicle of Philanthropy
www.philanthropy.com

The Non-Profit Times
http://www.nptimes.com

For Further Training

CharityChannel
http://charitychannel.com

The Grantsmanship Center
http://www.tgci.com

Appendix D—Suggested Reading

Ahern, Tom. *Seeing Through a Donor's Eyes: How to Make a Persuasive CASE for Everything from your Annual Drive to your Planned Giving Program to your Capital Campaign.* Medfield: Emerson and Church Publishers, 2009.

Andresen, Katya. *Robin Hood Marketing: Stealing Corporate Savvy to Sell Just Causes.* San Francisco: Jossey-Bass, 2006.

Barbato, Joseph. *Attracting the Attention Your Cause Deserves.* Medfield: Emerson and Church Publishers, 2005.

Bell, Jeane, Jan Masaoka and Steven Zimmerman. *Nonprofit Sustainability: Making Strategic Decisions for Financial Viability.* San Francisco: Jossey-Bass, 2010.

Daw, Jocelyne. *Cause Marketing for Nonprofits: Partner for Purpose, Passion, and Profits.* New York: John Wiley and Sons, Inc., 2006.

Drucker, Peter F.. *Managing the Nonprofit Organization: Principles and Practices.* New York: HarperCollins Publishers, 1990.

Eisenstein, Amy: *50 Asks in 50 Weeks: A Guide to Better Fundraising for Your Small Development Shop.* Rancho Santa Margarita: CharityChannel Press, 2010.

Grace, Kay Srinkel. *Fundraising Mistakes that Bedevil All Boards (And Staff Too): A 1-Hour Guide to Identifying and Overcoming Obstacles to your Success.* Medfield: Emerson and Church Publishers, 2004.

Lysakowski, Linda: *Fundraising as a Career: What, Are You Crazy?* Rancho Santa Margarita: CharityChannel Press, 2010.

Martin, Patricia. *Made Possible By: Succeeding with Sponsorship.* San Francisco: Jossey-Bass, 2004.

Olshansky, Norman and Linda Lysakowski, eds., *YOU and Your Nonprofit: Practical Advice and Tips from the CharityChannel Professional Community.* Rancho Santa Margarita: CharityChannel Press, 2011.

Stroman, M. Kent: *Asking about Asking: Mastering the Art of Conversational Fundraising.* Rancho Santa Margarita: CharityChannel Press, 2011.

Teitel, Martin. *"Thank You for Submitting Your Proposal": A Foundation Director Reveals What Happens Next.* Medfield: Emerson and Church Publishers, 2006.

Glossary

501(c)(3): An IRS designation given to nonprofit, tax-exempt organizations. Your organization's tax-exempt status will be explained in its IRS letter of determination.

990: The IRS tax form for tax-exempt organizations. 990's are filed every year.

990PF: The IRS tax forms for private foundations.

Brand: How an organization or person is recognized and thought of by the public. A reputation.

Branding: Activities you or your organization engage in to brand themselves or promote their brand.

Budget justification: A narrative explanation of your budget items describing how your costs were derived.

Cover letter: A letter accompanying every funding request that includes the purpose of your request and outlines what is included in your proposal package.

Executive summary: The first section of larger proposal narratives. Required for federal funding.

Exempt employee: An employee who is exempt from certain wage and hour laws, i.e., overtime pay. Usually salaried employees.

Fringe rate: The percentage of salary your organization pays for fringe benefits.

FTE: Full time equivalent. Used in the personnel budget to signal what portion of salary is being allocated to that program or funder.

G&A: General and administrative expenses. Commonly referred to as overhead expenses. G&A is usually expressed as a percentage of personnel and non-personnel expenses combined.

In-kind contributions: Non-cash contributions. In-kind contributions, although non-monetary in nature, are listed in your revenue and expense budgets as a monetary value.

Letter of Intent: A brief one to two page letter sent to a funder before the proposal. A letter of intent contains all the elements of the proposal, usually in one or two sentences per element.

Logic model: A one-table table that lays out your program goals, objectives, methodology and outcomes.

NOFA: Notice of Funding Availability. A document put out by funders, mainly governmental, to explain funding criteria and solicit applications.

Non-exempt employee: An employee who is not exempt from wage and hour laws, i.e., those defining overtime pay. Usually hourly employees.

RFP: Request for Proposals. A document that some funders circulate to receive grant requests.

Index

FUNDRAI$ING
as a Career

What, Are You Crazy?

www.charitychannel.com

50 A$KS
in 50 Weeks

A Guide to Better Fundraising for
Your Small Development Shop

www.charitychannel.com

ASKING
about Asking

Mastering the Art of
Conversational Fundraising™

www.charitychannel.com

*Charity*Channel
PRESS™

Just Released!

Capital Campaigns

Everything You NEED to Know

www.charitychannel.com

CPSIA information can be obtained at www.ICGtesting.com
Printed in the USA
BVOW041354270113

311654BV00006B/85/P